OPPORTUNITIES IN
Physician
Assistant Careers

TERENCE J. SACKS

D1495324

Foreword by
Ann L. Elderkin
Past President
American Academy of Physician Assistants

VGM Career Books

Chicago New York San Francisco Lisbon London Madrid Mexico City
Milan New Delhi San Juan Seoul Singapore Sydney Toronto

Library of Congress Cataloging-in-Publication Data

Sacks, Terence J.
    Opportunities in physician assistant careers / Terence J. Sacks ;
foreword by Ann L. Elderkin.
        p.   cm. — (VGM opportunities series)
    Includes bibliographical references.
    ISBN 0-07-138727-7 (hardcover)
    ISBN 0-07-138726-9 (paperback)
    1. Physicians' assistants—Vocational guidance.   I. Title.
II. Series.

R697.P45 S227   2002
610.69'53—dc21   2002016822

VGM Career Books

A Division of The **McGraw·Hill** Companies

3 4 5 6 7 8 9 0   DSH/DSH   0 1 0 9 8 7 6

ISBN 0-07-138727-7 (hardcover)
ISBN 0-07-138726-9 (paperback)

This book was set in Adobe Garamond by Rattray Design
Printed and bound by Lake Book Manufacturing

Cover photograph copyright © Digital Vision

McGraw-Hill books are available at special quantity discounts to use as
premiums and sales promotions, or for use in corporate training programs. For
more information, please write to the Director of Special Sales, Professional
Publishing, McGraw-Hill, Two Penn Plaza, New York, NY 10121-2298. Or
contact your local bookstore.

This book is printed on acid-free paper.

I dedicate this book to my wife, Mary Jane, my biggest booster and constant companion, whose ever-present support and good counsel have contributed more than anything else to whatever smidgen of success this book attains.

CONTENTS

FOREWORD

IT TAKES MORE than desire to become a physician assistant (PA). It takes determination to master the prerequisite college science courses. It takes foresight to gain the prerequisite clinical experience—as an emergency medical technician, medic, nurse, other health care worker, or volunteer. It takes stamina to survive two grueling years of course work and intensive clinical education. It takes compassion to help the women, men, and children who turn to you each day for critical answers. It takes teamwork to practice with other medical and health professionals. Practicing medicine as a physician assistant is a most rewarding profession.

People become physician assistants for a number of reasons. Some because they want to provide hands-on medical care but want to retain some flexibility in their personal lives rather than being the always on-call physician. Some because they are in another health profession and want more responsibility for the medical care of their patients.

I had always wanted to be in the health care field, but I was undecided about which profession I wanted to pursue until, about twenty years ago, I learned about the physician assistant profession. For me it was a means of providing day-to-day medical care to patients without spending the four years in medical school and the three years in a residency program required to become a physician.

I also liked the fact that PAs do not practice medicine independently. They work as a member of a team with a supervising physician. When I worked as a PA in primary care and surgery, I had the authority to make autonomous decisions about the care of patients—including writing prescriptions—and consulted with physicians if necessary. In most states the physician can be away from the practice while the PA is seeing patients.

Under state and federal health care reform, the demand for physician assistants is expected to grow. The U.S. Department of Labor projects a 48 percent increase in the number of jobs between 1998 and 2008. A survey of physician assistant school graduates revealed there were approximately six job offers for each graduate.

As you can see, the job prospects for physician assistants are good. The work is intense but rewarding. As you explore your future career options, consider the possibility of providing quality medical care as a physician assistant.

Ann L. Elderkin
Past President
American Academy of Physician Assistants

ACKNOWLEDGMENTS

IT TAKES THE contributions and assistance of many to create a book—any book—and this is certainly true of this book. But of the numerous people who were so generous with their time and support, a few are particularly deserving of mention—especially Kevin Bayes, Information Specialist, American Academy of Physician Assistants. Kevin responded to my every request for information and assistance with a speed and thoroughness that was nothing short of amazing.

Also contributing greatly in the completion of this book were Jan Towers, Ph.D., RN, of the American Academy of Nurse Practitioners; Kathryn Scott, B.S.N., RN, of the American Nurses Association; and the public relations staff of the American College of Nurse-Midwives.

I would like to acknowledge the tremendous assistance I received from all of those who so kindly consented for the interviews used in this book. They include: Kevin Kusch, student, Physician Assistant Program, Chicago Medical School, North Chicago; Larry Linder, Wanda Wynn, Myra Kemna, Pam Adams,

Susan Galloway, and Mort Krakow, all then physician assistant students at Cook County Hospital, Chicago; Julie Finn, Rod Full, Lynn Mulvey, and Mary Lou O'Keefe, all practicing physician assistants (Ms. O'Keefe is also a surgeon assistant); Barbara Clark; and Joyce Martin.

Thanks also to Kris Healy, PA-C, then Assistant Director, Physician Assistant Program, Cook County Hospital, Chicago; Scott Chavez, PA-C, Midwestern University Physician Assistant Program, Downers Grove, Illinois; and Michael Pagano, Ph.D., PA, Director, Physician Assistant Department, Chicago Medical School, North Chicago.

Also very helpful was Stephen Kuhn, then president of the Illinois Academy of Physician Assistants, Westmont, who was extremely accommodating in arranging the various interviews cited above.

I would certainly be ungrateful if I omitted the many fine suggestions and contributions of my editors, especially Denise Betts, Acquisitions Editor, and Betsy Lancefield, Editor, both of VGM Career Books.

Finally, I would like to express my gratitude to the entire reference department staff at the Skokie Public Library, Skokie, Illinois, who could not have been more accommodating in handling my various requests for assistance.

1

A NEW HEALTH CARE FIELD BEGINS

PHYSICIAN ASSISTANTS (PAs) have made amazing progress since the profession's inception in 1965. Today they function as the doctor's right-hand person, backup, or, in some cases, substitute. He or she is an important part of the health care team, so much so that the Congressional Office of Technical Assessment has described PAs as follows: "Within the limits of their expertise, PAs provide care that is the equivalent in quality to the care provided by physicians."

Though small in number—they account for less than 5 percent of the total number of physicians in the United States—physician assistants are in such demand that PA schools are hard pressed to meet that demand and now have roughly six to eight openings per graduate. And even as this book goes to press, more PA schools are opening all over the country.

Furthermore, PAs have had good acceptance from the public and physicians alike. True, there are some physicians practicing today who see PAs as a threat to their profession, but they are relatively few. The overwhelming majority of physicians in practice, especially the younger ones, are quite open to the profession and regard PAs as a possible solution to the long-term problems in health care of access to and maldistribution of physicians, particularly in inner city and rural areas.

Factors That Account for the Profession's Current Stature

How did PAs gain such status and acceptance in just a few decades? For one thing, as just noted, problems stemming from the maldistribution of physicians and lack of health care in certain parts of the population increasingly are causes for concern. This shortage is especially acute in rural areas and in the inner city. Nearly 20 percent of the U.S. population live in counties of fewer than fifty thousand people, but only 8 percent of all practicing physicians are located in these areas.

For another, Americans are placing higher value on health care. This is reflected in the news media—radio, TV, newspapers, and magazines —all of which have exposed millions of Americans to new drugs, new methods of treatment, and so forth and have created an ever-growing demand for medical services.

Primary care doctors (those to whom patients turn when they have health problems) in particular have felt the crunch and are working hard to get out from underneath. As the first line of defense in health care, they see everything from nosebleeds and bee stings to serious systemic disorders such as arthritis and diabetes. As such they are gatekeepers handling the bulk of health care problems that are presented and referring to specialists those cases that are more complex.

Today, in many cases, particularly in sparsely settled rural areas, the PA is often the medical professional to whom patients turn—the one to whom many Americans go when they seek medical care. Nonetheless, the supervising physician is ultimately in charge of the patient's care.

In the 1960s, when the first PA training program was developed at Duke University Medical Center, there was a similar shortage of doctors, particularly in the primary care area. The situation was made worse by a perpetual nursing shortage due to high turnover, a situation that has persisted, more or less, to the present day. At that time many also came to regard health care as a right, not simply a benefit, and they insisted that disenfranchised groups such as women, minorities, and the aged be guaranteed access to health care.

Why the Physician Shortage Today?

The shortage of medically trained doctors, especially in the primary care area, was underscored by the Report of the Surgeon General's Consultant Group on Medical Education. The report pinpointed three main reasons for the need for increased medical manpower:

1. rapid population forecasts, especially among the aged, who are historically the greatest users of health care services
2. increased use of health resources by all parts of the population for reasons including the widespread use of health insurance, particularly federally sponsored programs such

as Medicare (for the aged) and Medicaid (for the poor and needy); greater sophistication on the part of consumers; and a corresponding need for health care services

3. greater number of doctors needed for research, specialization, administration, and so forth

Although the number of physicians per 100,000 has remained fairly stable overall—roughly 141 per 100,000—the number of primary care physicians has dropped significantly.

In many cases the reason for this decline is economic. Primary care physicians deal in cognitive skills, those having to do with diagnosing disease, interpreting tests, taking medical histories, performing patient examinations, and so forth, while the skills of specialists, such as urologists and cardiologists, are more technical and involve more specialized knowledge. Such specialists are reimbursed at a rate higher than that for the primary care doctor. Thus, today, on average, a surgeon receives a salary of $236,000, whereas the primary care physician earns about $137,000.

In addition, students often regard specialization as more glamorous and exciting, dealing as it does with the latest results of technology and treatment. For all of these reasons, primary care physicians have been in short supply for several decades, and the shortage sees no sign of abating.

Origins of the PA Concept

In 1961 Dr. Charles L. Hudson, in his address to the American Medical Association, developed the concept of the physician assistant. He proposed that persons with no previous medical education be trained to perform such clinical tasks as suturing (stitching), IV treatments, and lumbar puncture, thus freeing up the physician for more complex tasks.

Hudson's proposal lay dormant for several years, but in 1965 two events occurred that helped shape the development of the profession. First, Dr. Henry Silver and Loretta Ford, RN, established a program at the University of Colorado that trained nurses with bachelor's degrees for child care treatment in clinics serving impoverished areas. The program later served as a prototype for nurse practitioner training (see Chapter 5).

However, the development with the most immediate impact on the profession was the establishment of a two-year program at Duke University Medical Center, Durham, North Carolina, to train physician assistants. Four ex-navy corps people from the Vietnam conflict were the first students enrolled.

The Duke program established two basic principles that since have guided the profession: (1) training would be relatively brief compared to medical school (nine months of basic science courses followed by fifteen months of clinical training); and (2) the physician assistant would serve in a supervised practice under the direction of the medical doctor.

The PA would be trained to take medical histories, look for symptoms that could prove helpful in determining diagnoses, do patient examinations, diagnose the patient's problem, perform medical tests, and take over some of the management of the patient's treatment. The program was not based on a nursing model, and tasks would not be performed independent of the supervising physician. Physician assistants would handle most, but not all, of the physician's duties.

Years of Growth and Expansion

Between 1965 and 1971 programs very similar to the Duke program were established at Bowman Gray School of Medicine (Wake Forest University, Winston-Salem, North Carolina), and at Oklahoma, Yale (New Haven, Connecticut), Alabama (Birmingham), George Washington (Washington, D.C.), Emory (Atlanta, Georgia), and Johns Hopkins (Baltimore, Maryland) universities. In addition, the department of surgery at the University of Alabama instituted the first special physician assistant program in 1967, emphasizing training in general surgery as well as in various surgical subspecialties.

In 1968 Alderson-Broaddus College in Philippi, West Virginia, combined a liberal arts education with physician assistant training to establish the first four-year degree program. Similar programs were begun shortly afterward at Northeastern University in Boston and at Mercy College in Detroit.

In 1969 the University of Washington School of Medicine, Seattle, introduced the Medical Extension (Medex) program, which featured three months of classroom instruction followed by twelve months of apprenticeship under a supervising physician, who presumably would hire the student upon completion of the program. By 1971 the Medex program had expanded to Los Angeles; Birmingham, Alabama; Salt Lake City, Utah; Hanover, New Hampshire; and Grand Forks, North Dakota.

Funding received from the federal government—which accepted the new profession almost from the start—under the Federal Health Manpower Act of 1971, doubled the number of training programs to more than 50 by 1974, and since then the profession has more than doubled again. Currently there are more than 120 programs that train PAs and an additional three that train surgeon assistants.

As a means of certifying the accomplishments of PA graduates to prospective employers, three schools (Duke, Bowman Gray, and the University of Texas at Galveston) joined together to offer the first voluntary certification examination for graduates in 1972. By 1973 this testing was taken over by the National Board of Medical Examiners, and its prestige and the increasing number of graduates drew 880 candidates to its first offering in December 1973. To this day, certification by national examination remains a basic foundation of the PA program. Currently it is administered by the National Commission on Certification of Physician Assistant Programs (NCCPA) and is open only to graduates of accredited PA programs.

To remain certified, PAs must complete one hundred hours of continuing medical education (CME) every two years. Every six years they must pass a recertification exam or complete an alternative program combining learning studies and a take-home exam.

The APAP Is Established

Another very important development that helped shape the new profession was the establishment in 1972 of the Association of Physician Assistant Programs (APAP), headquartered in Alexandria, Virginia. It serves physician assistant programs in much the same manner the Association of American Medical Colleges serves medical schools. It helps in curriculum development, in the exchange of information among schools, and in promoting continuing education.

The final step in the development of the certification program was some procedure to evaluate the new PA training programs to make sure they met certain basic standards. Here the National Academy of Sciences Board of Medicine recommended in 1970 that the American Medical Association, the Association of American Medical Colleges, and several federal agencies cooperate in developing standards for PA training programs. This function is now handled by the Accreditation Review Committee on Education for PAs.

A Look at the Profession Today

Following is a brief profile of more than 42,000 respondents of 44,000 physician assistants contacted in a 2000 survey of physician assistants:

Demographics
Gender: 45 percent male, 55 percent female
Average age: 41 years
Education: 83 percent have a four-year college degree,
    39.6 percent have a bachelor's degree, 39 percent have
    a bachelor's degree certified for physician assistant,
    27.5 percent have a master's degree, 2.3 percent have
    a doctorate

Practice Specialty
59.2 percent—primary care
36.5 percent—family practice
10 percent—internal medicine
7 percent—internal medicine subspecialties (cardiology,
    dermatology, allergy, etc.)
10 percent—emergency medicine
3 percent—obstetrics/gynecology

4 percent—pediatrics
20 percent—surgery
10 percent—other

Practice Setting
74 percent—outpatient setting
37 percent—solo or group practice
3 percent—HMO/managed care
11 percent—ambulatory care (public or private clinics, rural clinics, inner city clinics, or other clinic settings)
39 percent—inpatient settings
36.5 percent—public or private hospitals
3 percent—Veterans Administration

Patient Visits Per Day
22 outpatient visits
14 inpatient visits

Population Size of Practice Setting
29 percent of all PAs practice in towns of fewer than 50,000
5.8 percent—10,000 or fewer
16 percent—100,000 or fewer
50 percent—500,000 to 1,000,000
20 percent—1,000,000 or more

Geographic Distribution by U.S. Region
23.9 percent—Northeast
23.4 percent—Southeast
13.4 percent—South Central

20.1 percent—North Central
18.2 percent—West

Average Number of Years in Practice: 8.7
25 percent—3 years or fewer
16 percent—16 years or more

Average Number of Years in Current Job: 4.4
22 percent—less than 1 year
36 percent—1 to 3 years
4 percent—16 years or more

Average Number of Hours Worked Per Week: 42

Average Number of Hours on Call Per Week: 26

Average Annual Salary: $65,177

Average East/West Coast Salaries: $5,000 more
New graduate starting salary: $56,000 to $58,000

Jobs for Every New Graduate: 7

AAPA Members: 24,975

Number of PA Students in 120 Accredited PA Programs: 10,000

As you can see, PAs work in large metropolitan areas as well as in towns and hamlets of five thousand and fewer, and they enjoy good acceptance wherever they work. For one, the work PAs do frees up supervising physicians to give more time to patients with serious problems. Putting it another way, the work the PA performs allows doctors more time to practice the sophisticated medicine for which they are trained. And PAs provide health care coverage and services in rural and inner city areas that otherwise might not have such coverage. In 2000, 29 percent of all PAs practiced in towns of fewer than 50,000 and 31 percent in cities of more than 500,000.

Often patient waiting times have been reduced, examinations are done in a less hurried atmosphere, and both the doctor and the patient have more time to discuss questions and concerns. In short, many believe PAs have brought more personalized health care to populations that until recently had very little access to medical care.

PAs also offer strong backing to primary care physicians because more than 70 percent of all practicing PAs are in clinical practice in the primary care areas. These include family and general practice, emergency medicine, pediatrics, and obstetrics/gynecology.

From a very limited background and training, PAs have evolved to the point where today there are physician assistants working wherever doctors are to be found. They practice in nearly all medical specialties including dermatology, allergy, public health, hematology, radiology, physician rehabilitation, anesthesiology, otolaryngology, psychiatry, and many other specialties too numerous to list. More than 67 percent of all PAs provide support for primary care physicians; in addition 14 percent work in surgical specialties, including general, vascular, orthopedic, thoracic, cardiovascular, plastic, and more.

Patients have benefited as well. Since the training period for PAs is shorter and involves a much smaller cash outlay, the PA field attracts many who are interested in medicine, but who are unable or unwilling to attend medical school.

The average PA student is roughly four to six years older than the typical college freshman. The PA student's older age suggests that many PAs start their careers later in life, in many cases as a second career. Also, 72 percent of the students entering PA school have at least four years of college education and a bachelor's degree.

In addition, the vast majority of all students enrolling in PA schools have had some kind of health care experience. For example, 32.5 percent have had medical experience in the military, 33.5 percent have been nurses' aides or orderlies, 29 percent have worked as clinical technicians, 23.8 percent have worked as emergency medical technicians, and 8.5 percent have served as registered nurses. In many cases, this health care experience is required for acceptance into a training program, although PA schools are abandoning this requirement.

Because of the shorter training period and the smaller dollar commitment, the profession has attracted many who, though they want a medical career, do not want the long years of training involved in becoming a physician.

Where PAs Work

Originally, the PA was seen as practicing in both inner city and rural areas, where residents had long had limited access or almost no access to health care. Today, however, since physician assistants support all kinds of physicians, they are to be found working wherever physicians work: private practice, health maintenance programs, hospitals, satellite prisons, the military, nursing homes, industrial health clinics, and student health services, to name but a few.

Nearly 30 percent of physician assistants work in hospital settings, including those in veterans hospitals and in the public health service, and 20 percent work in government settings, including the military services and the coast guard, national guard, and federal prisons.

According to the AAPA, in 1999, 67 percent of all PAs were in private practice in the offices and clinics of physicians, dentists, or other health practitioners. The rest were primarily in public health clinics, nursing homes, prisons, home health care agencies, and in the Department of Veterans Affairs.

A recent survey of all doctors showed that they believed that delegating certain responsibilities would increase the quality of health care delivered to patients. In addition, many also believed that PAs have brought better and more personalized health care to populations that traditionally have been underserved or had only limited access to health care.

A Typical Workweek and Compensation

A normal workweek for a PA depends upon the setting. If you work for a hospital, there is a 35 percent likelihood that you will work a forty-one to fifty-hour workweek, and a 35 percent chance that you will work between thirty-one and forty hours a week. In an outpatient setting—clinic or group practice, or solo practice— the likelihood would be about 51 percent that your workweek would be between thirty-one and forty hours and 35 percent likely that you would work a forty-one to fifty-hour workweek. There is also a 13 percent chance that you would spend between one and ten hours on call a week and a 9 percent chance that you would work between eleven and twenty hours on call a week. But seen another way, the chances are excellent—about 60 percent—that you would *not* have to work any on-call hours per week. ("On call" means hours that you are required to be available for duty over and above your regular hours.)

Salaries for PAs likewise vary depending upon the state in which they practice, specialty (surgical specialties generally will make more than primary care), and the type of practice (whether hospital based, in a group practice, in a solo practice, or in a managed care facility such as a health maintenance organization). In 2000 the American Academy of Physician Assistants reported that the total income of PAs who were not employed by the government or who were self-employed and worked at least thirty-two hours a week was $68,757; the median was $65,177. The comparable mean for PAs who had been in clinical practice for less than a year was $58,297; the median salary was $56,977. The Bureau of Labor Statistics reported that in 1998 the median income of PAs was $47,090. The middle 50 percent earned between $25,110 and $71,450 a year, while the highest 10 percent earned more than $86,760 a year.

Working conditions are on the whole good, with most PAs working in climate controlled, well-lighted places. But if you intend to work in surgery, you may have to stand for long periods and do a considerable amount of walking.

Workweeks and work schedules vary according to where you work and usually match those of your supervising physician. A few emergency room PAs work twenty-four-hour shifts twice a week, and others may work three twelve-hour shifts per week.

These are just a few of the responsibilities that you will face as a PA, and though they may not be quite as overwhelming as those facing the physician for whom you work, they are nevertheless powerful. In the following chapters we will discuss the very considerable commitment you make in studying for a career as a PA and the barriers that you face in getting into PA school and financing your education. Although formidable, as you will see, they are by no means insurmountable.

2

GETTING INTO PA SCHOOL

GETTING INTO PA school and staying there is by no means easy. PA schools are very choosy about the students they select, as well they might be since many schools receive three or four applications per opening. Nevertheless, if you have the capabilities, the required courses and grades, and the motivation, you likely will be accepted into a PA program—perhaps not the one that is your first choice, but most likely your second or third.

Once accepted, you are facing about twenty-four months of intense medical training. This chapter will discuss all the steps you'll take from deciding on a PA program to, ultimately, becoming certified as a physician assistant. Chapter 3 will discuss how to finance your education.

Do You Have What It Takes to Succeed?

Before applying to PA school, you should first take an inventory of your personal attributes and do a bit of soul-searching. Do you have what it takes to succeed as a physician assistant? Do you have the intestinal fortitude to withstand the demands on your time and patience by adults and/or children who may be ravaged by disease and pain? Often patients can be extremely unreasonable in the demands they make upon you. Can you deal with such patients, many of whom may be venting their fears and frustrations on you? Can you keep your sense of cool and empathy in such difficult situations?

It would be easy to celebrate a patient's success in overcoming a debilitating and worrisome disease, thanks to a medication or treatment you may have prescribed. But do you have what it takes to sit by the side of a patient who is caught in the last throes of disease and who literally may be withering away before you?

These are real life and death situations that you and your supervising physician may have to face every day as part of your work. If you don't think you can manage it, then perhaps you should consider some other career involving science and people, such as laboratory science. If you are uncertain—and who knows for sure without trying—there are lots of things you can do right now to test the waters of this career.

1. Talk to some practicing physician assistants. If you don't know any, check with your guidance counselor or contact some of the schools listed in Appendix C to give you some leads. Try to find out what is involved in this kind of work, how PAs feel about the profession, and what skills and abilities are called for. Chances are that whomever you contact will be more than happy to discuss the work with you, so don't hesitate to take this step. Your guidance counselor also can recommend books, visuals, and video-

tapes on the field that may prove helpful in getting a handle on the work and what is involved in pursuing this career.

2. Assess your background in science and biology. You must have a good understanding of human anatomy and physiology (how the body's various systems function, what forces can affect them adversely, and so forth).

3. Determine how good you are with people. This work requires infinite amounts of patience, understanding, and tact. Dealing with patients who often are cranky and who take out their frustrations on you are all part of the work, and you must be able to keep your cool even under the most trying circumstances.

To help you get a better understanding of the profession, try working as a hospital orderly, in which you transport patients from one part of the hospital to the other, for example, from hospital room to surgery, the lab, or the physical therapy department and back. This is a good way to judge how well you will do in a real-life patient situation. You also might consider volunteering. The important thing is that you get experience actually working with patients to see how well you relate to them.

Choosing a PA Program

Now that you have completed your inventory and done some soul-searching, and you are more convinced than ever that working as a PA is for you, the next step is to apply to several physician assistant programs, which you will find are located all over the country. This way, if your first choice school rejects you, you still have one or two others to fall back on. PA schools can vary considerably in such things as entry requirements, curriculums, financial aid and other costs, and so forth, so make sure that the school you select is right for you. The *Physician Assistant Programs Directory*, which is updated annually, will give you valuable information in helping you choose which schools to apply to. (If your school does not have a copy, you can obtain one for $35 by writing to the Association of Physician Assistant Programs, whose address is provided in Appendix B.) To be listed in the directory, programs must meet the accreditation standards of the Accreditation Review Commission on the Education of Physician Assistants. This way you know that no matter which programs you are interested in, if they are listed, they are accredited and meet the AMA standards for physician assistant programs.

It's important to try to select schools that closely match your requirements. Some programs, for instance, are geared to individuals who have extensive medical or health care experience, while others accept students who have no medical experience or have just graduated from high school.

The location of a school also can be an important consideration. For example, some programs are located in rural areas because their primary mission is to serve rural areas; others are located in more metropolitan settings. Some school curriculums are more geared to primary care; others offer options for those who want to enter specialty practice. In addition, if you want or need to work while pursuing your PA education, many programs offer part-time options that allow you to spread out your studies over a longer period of time.

As you can see, choosing the right physician assistant program is very important. Contact any individual programs of interest and be sure to request specific information about admission requirements, the selection process, any required background experience, costs involved, and so forth.

Requirements of the PA Program

In 2000 there were 120 physician assistant programs in the United States, including three offering special programs for surgeon assistants. Programs are located at medical schools, medical centers, hospitals, two- and four-year colleges and universities, and one is offered through the armed forces. All involve classroom instruction as well as laboratory work, and in the second year, clinical practice working with patients.

In addition, there are about fifteen postgraduate programs that offer training for various specialties including surgery, orthopedics, emergency medicine, and so forth. All of these programs are found in the *Physician Assistant Programs Directory*.

As noted above, entrance requirements vary considerably from school to school. Most require that you have at least two years of college. Some require that you have a bachelor's degree, but most do not. However, more than 50 percent of all applicants to PA programs have college degrees, 5.6 percent have master's degrees, and 1.2 percent have doctoral degrees. There is little doubt that a college degree will make a difference in getting you into a school, even if that school does not specifically require it.

In addition to at least two years of college and some health care experience, (the specific amounts of experience usually are not spelled out), nearly all PA schools require that you have completed courses in biology, English, the humanities and social sciences, chemistry, college math, and psychology. Here again the minimum requirements and specific courses required vary considerably from school to school, so write to the schools you are interested in for their specific information.

When filling out application forms, make sure they are neatly typed, without smudges, crossovers, and so forth, and are assembled properly with letters of reference. The neatness and accuracy of your application form does a lot more than tell the admissions board if you are technically eligible or not; it also shows how thorough, neat, and accurate you are and the amount of time and effort you are willing to put into your education. Further, it offers strong hints as to your dedication and ability in a field that calls for painstaking thoroughness and neatness.

Application forms vary from school to school, but you should be prepared to supply information on your academic background, work experience, how you plan to finance your education, and your reasons for wishing to pursue a PA education.

Most application forms ask that you supply the admissions committee with a statement or essay explaining why you are seeking to enroll in the physician assistant program, what you can bring to the program, and what you expect to get out of it. This statement is very important because it gives the admissions committee a good indication of your character, your commitment to a PA education, and your suitability for the profession. Do a rough pencil draft first; then review, correct, and edit it until you are completely satisfied that the statement reflects your career aspirations and what you expect to get out of PA school.

Finally, make sure that you allow enough time to obtain all of the records and letters of reference that you will need, including your college and high school academic transcripts, proof of work experience, and SAT scores.

A word of caution about letters of recommendation: These are important and often can make the difference between being accepted in a program, or not. If your academic background is lacking a course or two to meet a school's minimum entrance requirements, a letter from one of your college professors pointing to your fine volunteer work or your achievements in such things as student government, sports, debate, or the high school orchestra often can help compensate for missing courses on your résumé.

But before you use someone as a reference, make sure that this is okay with him or her. This person may not want the bother of writing such a letter or, even worse, may not think that you merit such a letter. Also, make sure the person knows you well enough to be able to judge your suitability for PA training. Don't try to rope in someone who knows you only slightly. A letter from someone who does not know you well will probably offer little of any practical value.

The Admissions Procedure

Once you have filled out the application form and attached any necessary supporting materials, you are ready to send it to the admissions committee at the school or schools of your choice. If your application passes a preliminary screening, it will probably go through an in-depth faculty and staff review.

Your academic records, personal references, your personal statement, and, in some cases, your patient care experience and college entrance examination test scores are all carefully reviewed. If approved, you will be called to come in for a personal interview. Often any shortcomings in your record can be overcome with a good interview, so it is important that you put your best foot forward. The main purpose of the interview is to help the committee evaluate your seriousness in wanting to become a PA. Are you truly committed to helping patients? Or are your reasons for wanting to enter the field spurious and based on, say, prestige or the fact that your father or mother or some other close relative succeeded in this field?

Come to the interview dressed tastefully. This is no time to call attention to your clothes. Rather, the emphasis should be on your ability to answer the committee's questions. Don't worry if you don't know all of the answers; nobody does and if you are uncertain, don't guess or pretend. Just admit that you are uncertain of the answer and go on to the next question.

If all is in order and you are accepted, congratulations. You are on your way to becoming a physician assistant.

A Look at the PA Program

Now, let's look at the PA program itself. How long is the program and what kind of courses will you be expected to take? First, nearly all of the programs are two years in length and very intensive, running almost year-round with short breaks between semesters. In certain instances you may be expected to attend classes seven days a week, although this is rare and for short periods of time. Because of the rigorous demands of the program in terms of time (hours spent in class and in study), working after hours is probably not a good idea. You should be prepared to put forth your best efforts and concentrate on your studies and classroom work.

A typical program might offer a bachelor's degree, assuming that you have the minimum two years of college that is required.

A few programs are three to four years long, with the prerequisites becoming a part of the total program. Some schools award a certificate or an academic degree. Because of the depth and intensity of the curriculum, a growing number of schools are awarding the master's degree.

Just about all programs focus on didactic (classroom) instruction, laboratory sessions, and, during the second year, clinical rotations. The first year focuses on the basic sciences: microbiology, anatomy, physiology, pharmacology, and a few additional courses such as clinical medicine, medical ethics, and clinical lab. You also may have your first exposure to patients through courses covering physical examination, patient history taking, and physical diagnosis.

The second year can run from nine to fifteen months and includes clerkships and preceptorships (working with a doctor) in various settings, primarily in the hospital, but also in outpatient clinics, nursing homes, and so forth. Most programs include clinical rotations in primary care medicine—internal medicine, family practice, pediatrics, obstetrics/gynecology—as well as in other specialties such as psychiatry, emergency medicine, and geriatrics. You also could be expected to examine a patient, take his or her case history, come up with a tentative diagnosis, and prescribe a treatment, all of which will be reviewed by your instructors and associates.

Occasionally, one or more of these clerkships or rotations (they are basically the same) are served under the supervision of a physician who is seeking to hire a PA. Successful completion of such a rotation often can lead to a job offer.

Postgraduate specialty programs, as yet unaccredited, are offered in such areas as emergency medicine, pediatrics, neonatology, gynecology, critical care medicine, and occupational medicine, as well as surgery. But to qualify for postgraduate specialization, you must be a graduate of an accredited program certified by the National Commission on Certification of Physician Assistants (NCCPA).

Certification

Upon successful completion of a PA program, you are eligible to take the national certifying examination given by the NCCPA. Only those passing the test can use the title "Physician Assistant—Certified (PA-C)." In order to maintain certification, you must complete one hundred hours of continuing medical education (CME) every two years and take a recertification exam every six years. For a list of regulations and state laws applying to the PA practice, contact the American Academy of Physician Assistants.

Legal Status of the PA

The 1995 decision of the State of New Jersey to allow for the use of PAs under the supervision of a physician means that PAs can now practice in all fifty states. And since 1998, in forty-one states and the District of Columbia, PAs are allowed to prescribe medicine to patients, if authorized by the supervising physician.

Although PAs, like their supervising physicians, can be sued for malpractice, the fact is that the use of qualified physician assistants who perform within the limits of their authority as specified by the state in which they practice tends to reduce the risk of such malpractice suits.

In general, malpractice suits tend to arise from poor physician-patient relations rather than from outright negligence. And the evidence is mounting in study after study that where PAs are employed, patients receive more attention, waiting periods are shorter, and patient care and satisfaction are improved. This in turn cuts down on the likelihood of the patient suing the physician or PA.

If the physician or PA is sued for malpractice, the liability is shared by both. It is thus highly unlikely that the physician would allow his or her PAs to function beyond their training and experience or what the state law allows.

Real-Life Examples

To see how effective physician assistants can be in real-life situations, let's examine a few case histories that are based on actual careers:

Mary Weston works in a four-physician group practice in a small town in western Colorado. She says that in the three years that she has worked in the practice, only three or four patients have refused to see her. She attributes her acceptance with patients to the fine support she gets from the receptionist and front office staff, who take the time to explain to patients just what a PA is and what he or she does.

In many cases, Mary sees patients when they come in for a routine procedure. If, for example, a patient comes in for a Pap smear and the doctors are behind schedule, that patient may opt to see Mary instead. If this patient is pleased, she may decide to see Mary in future visits.

The doctor in charge of Mary's clinic freely admits that finances were a prime consideration in deciding to hire her. "We needed someone who could be responsible for visits to nursing home patients after the federal government reduced its reimbursements for such visits, and who would accept a lower salary than a medical doctor would."

Although supervision of PAs is somewhat of a burden in most medical practices, it is much less of a factor in Mary's case, where four doctors take turns supervising her work for one week a month each. In addition, the physician in charge notes that Mary follows a protocol that spells out the procedures that she should follow for various cases. So instead of having to suggest courses of treatment for each case presented, it is simply a matter of making sure that Mary follows the written protocol.

Mary's supervising physician contends that the group's success in using Mary is based on two factors: "Our work in creating a detailed protocol, which anticipates what Mary should do in just about all cases, and Mary's skill in adhering to the protocol."

Dr. Martin Arroyo has a solo family practice in a county in southwestern Texas where the unemployment rate is 40 percent and the average annual income per resident is about $4,000. Dr. Arroyo freely admits his inability to hire another physician to take some of the burden off of his shoulders. "We simply cannot afford another doctor, and even if we could, it would be just about impossible to find anyone willing to work under these economic conditions."

The obvious solution? Hire a PA. The PA receives about half of what an MD would get in pay and could handle most of the doctor's normal duties.

To pave the way for his new PA, Dr. Arroyo has posted a sign in his office outlining the fact that he works with a physician assistant. It details the PA's training and supervision. "Once people understand the concept, we have no problems in assigning them to see the PA."

In both cases cited above, the primary reasons for hiring the PA were financial. But both doctors have found to their delight that the practice did not suffer in quality. In fact some patients actually preferred to see the PA. Some physicians who work with PAs give their patients a choice of whom to see. In most instances, appointments with PAs are easier to obtain.

At one time Dr. John Bates, a physician with a solo practice in a tiny community of fifteen hundred in southern Indiana, was being swamped with forty or so patients who flooded his office daily. He was putting in long hours, from 10:00 A.M. to 7:30 or 8:00 P.M. every day, which did not help his home life. Today, however, Dr. Bates is seeing more patients each day—about sixty-five—but he usually manages to get home by 5:30 or 6:00 P.M.

How did he do it? Not by adding a partner, but by hiring Cliff Finch, PA. Like hundreds of other physicians throughout the country, Dr. Bates is finding that hiring a PA can help increase the patient volume without increasing the practice costs as much as does adding a new physician.

In rural areas, PAs can make a difference between a practice that is profitable and one that is not. But the biggest advantage is in relieving physician stress. If stress is the problem, says Dr. Bates, hiring a PA who can take over such tasks as taking histories, preparing charts, treating minor problems, and assisting in surgery is a real plus.

In the examples cited above, we have seen how the addition of PAs to a practice is paying off in many ways unforeseen when the first programs were established in 1965. Now let's look at what is involved in funding a physician assistant education program.

3

PAYING FOR YOUR EDUCATION

PAYING FOR AN education as a physician assistant is expensive. A 2000 survey of PA programs shows that the average cost of tuition for in-state students was $28,800 per year. For out-of-state students costs were considerably higher, averaging $34,800, because by law, schools are required to give preference to in-state students, and they have budgeted to offer such preference through reduced tuition.

Although tuition costs cover the entire length of the program per year, they do not include books, supplies, lab fees, and living expenses such as room and board, all of which can add thousands of additional dollars to the cost of education. Since all tuition fees quoted are approximate and subject to change, it is best to check with the specific school in which you are interested for up-to-date costs. Keep in mind that tuition in 2000 ranged anywhere from $4,000 to $75,000. Tuition for a public school is always much less expensive than that for a private school.

Financial Aid

Although a PA education is undoubtedly expensive, paying for it is definitely possible. In fact, most students attending PA school carry a combination of loans received from various sources, scholarships, and grants in order to pay for their education.

Money is available, but you will have to work hard to find it. It will not fall into your lap. Once accepted by a PA program, your real work begins. Check first with your school's office of financial assistance, which exists primarily to help students who would otherwise be unable to meet the costs of their education. (That includes most students attending PA schools!)

At your school's financial aid office, you can receive information on grants, loans, and other assistance available from a variety of sources. In fact, you can apply for some financial aid programs only through the financial aid office. Even though the financial aid office can provide information and perhaps the required forms, it is up to you to gather the information related to various loan and scholarship programs and to fill out the forms and meet deadlines.

Similarly, the burden of meeting the costs of your PA education rests on you and your family. Your school, through the financial aid office, may pay the difference between what you are able to pay and the actual cost of the program.

To keep costs as low as possible, you might consider living at home rather than at school. This may lower your living costs considerably, but then again it may add more problems than it's worth. For instance, will it add considerable commuting time to your schedule, time that could be used much more profitably in study?

Also, will you be able to study at home, or will there be too much noise and too many distractions? And what about transportation (public transportation versus owning your own car), food, and personal expenses? You must plan, budget, and above all, read thoroughly the financial assistance materials available and follow the instructions to the letter.

Government Assistance

Federal sources of financial assistance include various loans and grants guaranteed by the federal government but offered in some cases through the state. There are several such programs including the Stafford Student Loans (formerly known as the Guaranteed Student Loan program), HEAL (Health Education Assistance Loan), National Defense Student Loans, SLS/Plus (Supplementary Loans for Students/Plus), and others.

These programs vary a lot in such fundamental areas as borrowing limits, interest rates, when interest is to start accruing, deferments, and so forth. It is therefore extremely important that you apply for the programs that are best for you, assuming that they are available through your school. Besides consulting with your financial aid office, you can also write the Consumer Information Center, *Student Guide*, Pueblo, Colorado 81009 for a free catalog (#578W).

Then, too, each state has an agency that guarantees student loans. In Illinois, for example, it is the Illinois State Scholarship Commission. Some states offer their own educational assistance programs of loans or grants through the state loan agency.

Don't forget that you must apply for financial assistance annually; it does not carry over from year to year. Your application for financial assistance, from whatever source, is carefully reviewed by the agency in question on the basis of income, assets, family size, and other information, not just for you, but for your spouse and parents as well. Your application for assistance most likely will be answered within four to six weeks of your needs assessment, as compiled by the College Scholarship Services.

It is this needs assessment that will determine your eligibility for federal and state financial assistance, so it is very important that you fill out any required forms as accurately as possible and that you supply all of the information called for.

In filling out application forms, read the instructions carefully. If you use estimates, you may have to prove their accuracy. Also, you will have to submit a copy of your most recent IRS 1040 Income Tax Return and, most likely, so will your parents. Forms not completed as required may be returned, causing unnecessary delays and even forfeiture of your financial assistance award.

Finally, whether or not you receive financial aid will often depend upon circumstances beyond your control. For instance, your school's default rate may affect future funding from that institution, meaning that the school may not be able to award funds from a given federal loan source if the student default rates are too high. Then, too, prior academic degrees or previous years' earnings may disqualify you from funding, and deadlines for submitting your application for the current year may have passed by the time you apply.

Other Sources of Assistance

The paragraphs that follow list several scholarships, loans, and grants available specifically for physician assistant students and for college teachers in designated health care professions.

Physician Assistant Foundation (PAF)

The charitable arm of the American Academy of Physician Assistants, the PAF provides scholarships for PA students who are currently attending physician assistant school and who are members of the AAPA. Scholarship awards begin at $2,000. Applications can be submitted starting in the fall of the current year until the deadline—February 2 of the following year. Recipients are judged by committee, and applicants are notified and funds distributed by mid-May. For a current application form, contact your program director or the PAF at 950 North Washington Street, Alexandria, Virginia 22314.

Association of Physician Assistants in Cardiovascular Surgery (APACVS)

APACVS offers scholarships to second-year PA students who are interested in cardiovascular surgery and who are members of the APACVS. Scholarships are based on need, scholastic excellence, and a narrative describing your commitment to and qualifications for cardiovascular surgery. Contact APACVS at P.O. Box 4834, Englewood, Colorado 80111.

Commissioned Officer Student Training and Extern Program (COSTEP)

The Public Health Service assigns students in the health professions to work with one of eight public health service agencies. Assignments include various jobs and duties that range from research to clinical services. Students, commissioned as ensigns in the Public Health Service, serve from 31 to 120 days per assignment at a salary (based on 1999 figures) of approximately $2,100 per month.

Assignments also carry minimal health care benefits and military exchange commissary privileges. Students can list geographic and program preferences among a wide choice of challenging job opportunities that exist throughout the United States. Contact the Junior Commissioned Officer Student Training and Extern Program at 5600 Fishers Lane, Rockville, Maryland 20957-0001.

United States Navy-Health Services Collegiate Program (HSCP)

HSCP is aimed at providing financial incentives for college students in designated health care professions while they complete requirements for a bachelor's degree. Upon graduation you will obtain a reserve commission as a physician assistant in the Medical Service Corps, U.S. Navy. For more information and an application package, contact your local navy medical department recruiter.

Indian Health Service (IHS)

IHS scholarships offer financial support for students enrolled in health professions and allied health professions programs. Recipients incur a one-year service obligation to the IHS for each year of scholarship support received with a minimum period of service of two years. Non-Indian students may apply but priority is given to Indian applicants. Contact the Indian Health Service scholarship office at 301-443-6197.

Community Scholarship Program

Several states have been chosen by the federal government to participate in this fairly new program. Under the program, a community will sponsor a student to go to PA school in exchange for a commitment from the student to practice in the sponsoring community after completing his or her education. See Appendix A for a list of states participating in the program. They, in turn, will put you in touch with communities interested in sponsoring a PA.

National Health Service Corps Scholarship and Loan Repayment Program

This program is available to all PA students and graduates who agree to practice in a designated health shortage area for at least two years.

Scholarships

Scholars receive twelve monthly stipends of $796, plus an additional payment to cover other reasonable educational expenses, and payment to the school for tuition and required fees. For each year of the award, scholars incur one year of obligatory full-time primary health service at health care facilities in a Health Professional Shortage Area (HPSA) after graduation. For application forms write to the National Health Service Corps Scholarships, 2870 Chain Bridge Road, Suite 450, Vienna, Virginia 22182.

Loan Repayment

To qualify, you must be a graduate or a senior student who agrees to practice full-time in an approved loan repayment site. The program pays up to $50,000 in educational loans for a two-year commitment, $85,000 for a three-year commitment, or $120,000 for a four-year commitment. Payments are offered for qualified government and commercial educational loans. The program pays an additional amount equal to 39 percent of the payoff amount to cover federal, state, and local income taxes caused by government payments. For applications write to the NHSC Loan Repayment Program, 2870 Chain Bridge Road, Suite 450, Vienna, Virginia 22182.

New York Life Foundation Scholarship Program for Women in the Health Professions

This scholarship was established to assist mature women seeking the education required for entry into or advancement within a career in the health care field. Based on financial need, these scholarships are awarded for a year to cover tuition, fees, and school-related expenses such as child care and transportation. You must be a U.S. citizen, at least twenty-five years of age, and within twenty-four months of graduation to qualify. Grants range from $500 to $1,000 for full- or part-time programs, but they do not cover study at graduate or doctoral levels. Application forms are available January 1 through April 1 and are due April 15. Applications can be obtained by sending a self-addressed envelope with two first-class stamps to Business and Professional Women's Foundation, New York Life Foundation Scholarship Program, 2012 Massachusetts Avenue NW, Washington, D.C. 20036.

Constituent Chapters (State PA Associations)

State PA associations often provide scholarships for PA students based on financial need and academic ability. See Appendix E for a list of chapters.

Teri Supplemental Loan Program

A long-term loan with no needs requirement, this loan is intended for students and their families who require financing beyond that available from federally approved programs. A loan consolidation program is available. For an application call 800-255-TERI.

Publications

Some organizations that publish current information on scholarship and loan programs available to college students are provided below:

- The American Academy of Physician Assistants publishes a regularly updated financial aid booklet. The booklet lists sources of scholarships, grants, and loans. Write the AAPA at 950 North Washington Street, Alexandria, Virginia 22314-1552.
- Octameron Associates publishes many books and guides on college financial assistance and how to get it. For a catalog write to Octameron Associates, P.O. Box 2748, Alexandria, Virginia 22301.
- American College Testing publishes the *Financial Aid Need Estimator* to assist students in planning how to meet educational expenses. A report, customized for the student, includes the estimated family contribution, college costs, admission information, and state aid programs: $7.50 for mail service, $10.50 for fax service. To receive the *Estimator* form, write to American College Testing Program, P.O. Box 4029, Iowa City, Iowa 52243-4029.
- *Need a Lift* is the name of a 129-page booklet published annually by the American Legion that contains information on loans and scholarships. Send $3.00 to the American Legion, Attention: Emblem Sales, P.O. Box 1050, Indianapolis, Indiana 46206.

- College Board Publications produces a brochure entitled *Meeting College Costs*, which can help you estimate how much your family will need to contribute to college expenses. It is available free from College Board Publications, P.O. Box 886, New York, New York 10101.
- Garrett Park Press publishes several financial aid books dealing with health careers. One book, *Financial Aid for Minorities in Health Fields*, costs $5.95. Booklets in its "Dollars for College" series cover medicine, dentistry, nursing, and other fields. They sell for $6.95 each. Write to Garrett Park Press, P.O. Box 190, Garrett Park, Maryland 20896.
- National Scholarship Research Service publishes several useful guides and offers a financial aid computer service. For more information contact the National Scholarship Research Service, 2280 Airport Boulevard, Santa Rosa, California 95403.

Sources for Minorities

The National Association for the Advancement of Colored People (NAACP) offers a number of needs-based awards to minority students who show academic excellence and community involvement. An outstanding financial resource guide is available from NAACP, 4805 Mount Hope Drive, Baltimore, Maryland 21215-32987.

Other Sources

Civic, fraternal, and service organizations such as Lions Clubs, Kiwanis, and Rotary International often offer financial assistance—both scholarships and loans—based on financial need and academic excellence. Other organizations include the American Legion, Elks, Girl Scouts, Optimists, National Organization for Women (NOW), Jaycees, Civitan, AMVETS, and Business & Professional Women's Foundation. For more information check the white pages of your local phone directory or contact your local chamber of commerce.

In addition, organizations of all major denominations—Catholic, Protestant, and Jewish, for example—often provide grants or scholarships to members of their congregations or denominations. For more information talk with your rabbi, minister, or priest or contact the denomination's national office or a college financial aid officer.

Various ethnic organizations also might offer educational assistance to students of the same ethnic origin. If you are interested, check with your college financial aid officer for the name of the ethnic group that might apply.

Finally, don't overlook the company where your parents work. Employers often sponsor scholarship programs for their employees and/or their children. Inquire directly with the company, institution, military service personnel, or human resources department.

You also can contact the U.S. Department of Education Hot Line for answers to questions about financial assistance by staff trained in the complexities of the federal assistance program. Call (800) 433-3243 between the hours of 9:00 A.M. and 5:00 P.M. E.S.T.

4

ONE FIELD, FOUR DIFFERENT PROFILES

Older Student Entering a PA Program

Even as a teenager, forty-three-year-old Gary was interested in health care, working weekends and summers as a lifeguard while he was in high school. After school he became first a fireman and then an emergency medical technician, or paramedic. But he wanted to do more.

Because of his age, Gary thought he'd never be able to get into medical school. Then, through a friend, he heard about physician assistants (PAs). He learned that oftentimes the PA is the first primary health care professional you see for checkups or when you become ill—before you see the family practitioner, the pediatrician, or the obstetrician-gynecologist.

That sounded good to Gary, so he called the American Medical Association (AMA) to find out whom to contact and what was involved in qualifying as a physician assistant. From the AMA he received a list of colleges and universities that had PA programs.

He applied to seven or eight programs that he found interesting and was accepted by three, despite his age. He decided on a school in Chicago because that was where most of his family—including several brothers and sisters and his own immediate family—lived. The school's educational program was brand new, so Gary compared it with several other schools in the area offering the two-year certificate. The school he selected also offered a two-year program culminating in a bachelor's degree, for those with two or more years of college completed before enrolling in the PA program.

Gary's class was composed of an interesting mix of students, including several young women ages twenty-one to twenty-five, two students who were in their early thirties, and one who was about thirty-five. Most had their bachelor's degrees, although it is not required at his school.

Gary's first year of school was primarily basic science. The students took a gross anatomy course (among others), just like medical students do, and right from the start they worked on the body of a deceased for about eight weeks. "You may think you'd be squeamish, but this evaporates almost immediately once you start working on a cadaver," he explains. "You don't even think about it after a few minutes."

Nonetheless, after completing his first year of studies, Gary had to admit that there were days when he wondered why he ever entered the PA program. As he put it: "It was pretty rough. There were days, right from the start, when we were covering material that was very advanced. Even medical students shook their heads when they saw what we had to take."

Then there's the stress involved. "If you can't handle stress, the program is not for you," says Gary. At one point he was in class Saturdays and Sundays, so he and his classmates were in school seven days a week from about 9:00 A.M. to 4:30 P.M. There was very little time off—only a week or two between quarters—and the classes were held year-round.

Gary likens his position in school to that of residents. "When we begin our rotations through the various primary care departments," he says, "we'll be on call one day in four just like the residents are."

Right now, Gary thinks that he would like to focus either on emergency medicine or family practice. He likes emergency medicine because, as he puts it, "It gets the adrenaline going. It's fast moving and exciting." In addition, there's almost always something going on, and from his experience as a fireman, Gary is used to being confronted with one emergency situation after another.

Family practice appeals to him because it offers a chance to see a variety of patients. Soon Gary will be starting his rotations in several primary areas of medicine—obstetrics/gynecology, pediatrics, general practice, and surgery—and he is looking forward to that.

Once he's completed his studies, Gary will be required to take a test given by a national certification board, in which he will be questioned intensively about all the material covered in the PA program. There was formerly a practical component of the exam, but it was dropped because it overlaps to a great extent with the work students do in their second year of school. Students have about six months after they complete the PA program to take the certifying exam, and they can practice only if they pass.

Gary is well aware that to maintain his certification status, he will have to pass a certifying exam every six years; physician assistants are the only medical group with such a requirement. It was the PAs themselves who were responsible for making this certification a requirement in the belief that understanding medicine is a continuous process requiring constant study to keep abreast of what is happening.

Gary knows that there is no lack of opportunities in this profession. There are six to eight job possibilities for every graduate. As for working with doctors, Gary believes that the "vast majority accept you for what you are and realize that you are helping to free them up from some of their load." But he also knows that there are a few physicians who insist that you are not qualified to handle medicine until you have put in all of the time required to become a physician. As for the patients themselves, Gary has found that most accept PAs gladly and feel they can talk to PAs more readily than they can to their own doctors.

Right now the prospects for PAs are excellent, especially in the military. The air force, for example, will start you at a salary of roughly $45,000 a year if you agree to serve in this branch of the armed forces for two years. But most graduates will undoubtedly go into practice in rural or inner city areas, where the need is the greatest and where PAs can practice with the greatest autonomy.

Dermatology Specialist

Now let's switch to thirty-five-year-old Pam Morris, a PA working for a physician who runs a dermatology (skin disease) clinic in a west Chicago suburb.

In her clinic, Pam explains, new patients with skin problems first see the doctor, who takes their medical history and examines them. In most cases the patient then undergoes a routine work up. When

Pam sees "routine work up" on a chart, she immediately knows what tests are to be performed—ultrasound, physical examinations, or biopsies, for example—and she schedules the patients for the tests and makes sure that the tests are carried out. As a physician assistant Pam is licensed to practice medicine under the supervision of a physician in any of the fifty states. She estimates that she can handle 80 to 90 percent of the cases that physicians see with no problem. When all of the tests are completed, the patient again sees the doctor, who decides on the overall course of treatment.

Even though she works in a highly specialized field of medicine—dermatology—Pam believes that because of her training and experience she can handle most of the patients who present themselves to the dermatologist's office. "I am in a real specialty, so what I do some other physician assistants would not be able to handle. Likewise, I would never work under a thoracic surgeon or a urologist or some doctor with a very limited specialty, unless I was trained to do so."

In dermatology the problems are often emotional as well as medical, particularly in the case of teenagers, who are quite sensitive about facial blemishes. Although many patients are anxiety driven, there is almost always some overriding physical problem causing the rash, blemish, or other problem. As a physician assistant, Pam is involved in the same kinds of diagnostic and treatment patterns as her supervising physician, but on a more limited basis.

But Pam's current position is quite different from the one that she entered when she first finished physician assistant school in 1980. At that time, Pam worked in an inner city clinic where she had her own list of patients to see.

"These appointments were all for my own patients. They would come in, and if I were doing a well-baby check and I detected a heart murmur, for instance, I would call in the doctor I worked for to have him or her check the murmur and help me decide on how to treat such abnormal symptoms."

Pam noted that while she worked at the inner city clinic, she treated many patients who had conditions she was familiar with, for example, hypertension or high blood pressure. Consequently, she was confident in deciding on the course of treatment, but always subject to her supervising physician's review and approval.

While still functioning under the supervising physician's review, she explained, the physician assistant often can prescribe medication if he or she knows what the preferences of the physician in charge are in such cases. "The physician need not be with you when you see the patient. He or she may be in the building," she explains, "but if not, he or she is always available as telephone backup."

Still later, when Pam worked in a large city medical center, following her stint in the inner city clinic, she functioned as any staff physician would. "I would often take the patient history, do the physical, and handle orders for treatment and therapy, which would always be countersigned by my supervising physicians within a certain period of time, be that twenty-four hours or whatever."

In certain rural clinics in sparsely populated areas, she notes, the physician assistant quite often may serve as the primary provider of medical care—examining patients, ordering tests and medications, prescribing treatment, and doing whatever is required to treat the patient.

In some cases the supervising physician may be several hundred miles away and may only visit the clinic monthly, but in all cases he or she is always available on the telephone if the PA runs into a situation where he or she is uncertain of the proper treatment.

To become a physician assistant, Pam was trained in much the same manner as is a family physician, but on a more limited scale. For the first year of the two-year program, she was indoctrinated in the basic sciences, taking courses such as physiology, microbiology, pathology, anatomy, and pharmacology—the same courses medical students take. In fact she often had medical students sitting next to her taking the same classes. She also had her first exposure to clinical medicine, learning how to take notes, how to do a patient history, and how to do a patient examination.

The second year was spent going through the various medical rotations, in which she spent six to eight weeks each working in a hospital in a variety of primary medical fields that included obstetrics/gynecology, surgery, internal medicine, pediatrics, and family practice. "In physician assistant school, you are trained in primary care medicine. By primary care, I mean in those areas of medicine where you are most likely to see a doctor first. Although you are trained in various areas of medicine during this period, when you finish school, you are basically a family practitioner, the same as the medical students before they complete their residency."

She explained that it is during the students' residencies that they receive specific training in their specialty, be it in internal medicine, cardiology, allergy, or, as in Pam's case, dermatology.

Pam, who has been working since 1980, loves her profession. At first she regretted not being able, for financial reasons, to go to medical school when she was younger, but now she is happy that she did not. "Now I have a family including a baby, and I work long hours and I have a lot of responsibilities. But still it's not my own practice. I'd have a lot more headaches and responsibilities if I had my own practice."

Surgeon Assistant in Private Practice

Not all physician assistants go into primary care medicine. Many work as surgery assistants, as does Diane Wagner, forty-eight, who works in Chicago as a surgeon assistant. A surgeon assistant, she explains, is a person who has completed the physician assistant program and has had special training and/or experience to assist in surgery.

And that Diane has in abundance. For eleven years she worked as a surgical nurse and eventually was in charge of surgical personnel during the evening shift of a large Chicago hospital. She had a very responsible job, but felt like something was lacking. Although she would see patients in surgery, there was little, if any, contact with them prior to or after the surgery.

Through a friend she heard of the PA program. This seemed to offer the missing component of patient contact in her work that she was seeking.

At the time, Illinois had no physician assistant training programs. Instead, she trained for the PA position through a preceptorship, whereby she worked under a licensed physician in a kind of apprenticeship, but on a professional, medical level. Her preceptorship was four years in duration. Upon completion and with her preceptor's sponsorship, she was able to become a licensed PA, and she continues to work for him to this day.

"In our profession you do what the physician does," is the way she puts it. "I assist in surgery, I make rounds—the same as any other physician. I'm not a scrub technician or circulating nurse. I suture (stitch) patients, I retract, and I do things to make the operation easier to perform. Some surgeon assistants may open and close. In cardiovascular surgery there are surgeon assistants who harvest (take) veins from the legs, which are then used in bypass surgery. As a surgeon assistant I do the history and often counsel patients. I initiate orders for medicine, tests, or special treatments such as physical therapy or occupational therapy."

After eleven years in surgical nursing, Diane is very happy that she trained to become a PA. "It is extremely gratifying to be able to see patients from the inception of their problem, follow them through surgery until they are discharged from the hospital, and then see them for follow-up treatment and counsel at the office."

PA Employed in a State Prison

Finally, we come to Don Buehl, fifty-five, who works in yet another very unique and fulfilling job as a PA at Stateville Prison, near Joliet, Illinois. After working as an X-ray and laboratory technician for nearly fifteen years, Don learned about the PA program while reading the *Journal of the American Medical Association.* He found himself attracted to the work because, as he explains, "I wanted something offering greater responsibility and more patient contact."

A graduate of the first PA program established in the nation, at Duke University in 1973, he became affiliated with a practice in a small community of five thousand about seventy miles from Chicago, where for fifteen years he worked for a general (family) practitioner.

Since 1988, Don has been employed by a contractor who provides medical services for the State of Illinois Department of Corrections in Joliet. His work is part of the reception and classification procedure for all new inmates entering the system. Don's main job is to examine and make physical assessments of the health of all inmates assigned to the department of corrections for the northern half of the state. If, for example, an inmate suffers from a chronic disease such as arthritis, diabetes, or a heart condition, Don reviews what treatments that inmate is currently undergoing to deal with or to control the condition.

Then he sees to it that the patient follows the prescribed treatment as long as he remains in Joliet. When a patient is transferred out of Joliet to the receiving prison, the physician there will reassess the information Don has compiled and either will continue the treatment as prescribed or will order some other treatment or medication.

Although Don often sees as many as thirty patients a day, he finds the work stimulating—never boring or monotonous. "Every day is a new one, and you never quite know what you are going to run into. I see the inmates, assess their health, and decide what treatment, medication, and so forth will be appropriate for them. It's an unusual place to work in, but I really have learned to like it."

The PA Today

We've looked at four portraits of the work done by four very different PAs who, although they are not physicians, handle the vast majority of procedures that a physician would otherwise perform. They are part of the more than forty-two thousand physician assistants practicing all over the United States today. The profession is one of the fastest growing in this country, one that has more than tripled from twelve thousand practitioners in 1980. The Office of Technical Assessment has listed it as one of the twenty-five most promising career areas.

As for the specific duties physician assistants can perform, this will depend upon two factors: the supervising physician and state law. The American Academy of Physician Assistants lists several functions that are typically performed by PAs as follows:

taking medical histories
performing physical exams
ordering lab tests
diagnosing and treating illnesses
counseling patients
promoting wellness
assisting in surgery

This list is by no means all-inclusive, and there are many other duties that a supervising physician would want his or her PA to handle, so it would be a good idea to check the laws and regulations of the state in which you wish to practice first.

Nurse Practitioner

One further note: There is one other kind of practitioner whose work is very close to that of the physician assistant—the nurse practitioner. Nurse practitioners examine patients, recommend medications, order tests, and prescribe treatments, just as physician assistants do. Both are often called physician extenders, since they enable the physician to handle a much greater number of patients than would otherwise be possible. However, their approach and their training are slightly different. Chapter 5 compares the roles played by nurse practitioners and physician assistants, examining not only their similarities, but their differences as well, which are subtle but important.

5

ADVANCED PRACTICE NURSES

SHIRLEY WILSON-NOBLE cares for children with nosebleeds and elderly people with bleeding ulcers or high blood pressure, to name but a few of the kinds of disorders that she sees daily. She is not a physician assistant, she is a nurse practitioner (NP), one of nearly eighty-eight thousand NPs practicing in all parts of the country.

Mary Lu Dimond offers well-woman gynecological treatment and delivers babies at a large medical center in Cleveland. She is a certified nurse-midwife.

Finally, Jane Plotner is in charge of specialists who anesthetize patients at a large teaching hospital in suburban Los Angeles. She is a registered nurse-anesthetist, one of a group of medical professionals who are currently managing about 65 percent of the anesthetics administered in the United States, a figure that is probably closer to 85 percent of anesthetics administered in many rural sections.

These three women are part of an elite corps of nurses who have had from one and a half to two years of study over and above their basic two to four years of training as nurses. All are registered nurses. They and yet another group of nurses—clinical nurse specialists—handle many of the patients who visit the offices of primary care physicians. They are the first line of defense in the treatment of disease, and those to whom patients are most likely to turn when they become ill. In this chapter we will define what the nurse practitioner is and does and how he or she differs from the physician assistant.

Nurse Practitioners Focus on Primary Care

Nurse practitioners (NPs), like their colleagues and often their associates, physician assistants, are trained primarily as generalists. They work as primary care practitioners in handling the run-of-the-mill problems that cause patients to seek medical care. However, they also may concentrate in several areas of advanced nursing: family care, pediatrics, school nursing, women's health, geriatrics (working with the elderly), and occupational health, for example.

Advanced Practice Specialists

Nurse anesthetists, nurse-midwives, and clinical nurse specialists, on the other hand, are all specialists who are trained to work with patients who require special treatment. They, together with nurse practitioners, are advanced practice nurses who because of their training are qualified to handle patients with a variety of ills and health problems. Unlike physician assistants, they often work independently and have a collaborative relationship with physicians.

How NPs and PAs Differ and How They Are Alike

Virginia Trotter-Betts, past president of the American Nurses Association, notes that the curriculum for nurse practitioners and for nurse specialists centers on areas such as prevention, counseling, and well care, areas that also are emphasized in physician assistant programs. "Nurse practitioners don't want to be doctors," is the way she puts it. "They have their own agenda, one that can bring an additional perspective to a doctor's office."

Nurse practitioners can guide patients toward less expensive care, including self-care and steps to take to guard against illness. Virginia sees patients as turning increasingly to visiting nurse practitioners and other nurse specialists in schools, at work sites, in day-care centers, at community clinics, and in homes.

But despite their differences in approach, advanced practice nurses, especially nurse practitioners, handle many of the same patient problems that PAs do, and they often provide the same treatments, including:

- performing physical examinations and taking patient histories
- prescribing and managing medications for common or acute conditions
- managing chronic health problems and conditions such as diabetes, arthritis, high blood pressure, and depression
- evaluating and treating common symptoms of acute illnesses such as colds, infections, and asthma
- offering prenatal care, family planning, and management and delivery of normal pregnancies

- handling screening and preventive services, including blood pressure screening, nutrition counseling, immunization, and quit-smoking campaigns
- identifying conditions or problems requiring the services of a specialist

Groups That Comprise Advanced Practice Nursing

Here is a brief description of each of the four nursing groups found within the field of advanced practice nursing.

Nurse Practitioner

Number: There were approximately eighty-eight thousand clinically practicing NPs in 2000.

Education: Most of the estimated three hundred NP education programs in the United States today offer the master's degree. Nurse practitioners are eligible to practice in all fifty states and the District of Columbia as well as the territories; in at least thirty-six states, nurse practitioners are required to be nationally certified by the American Nurses Association or a specialty nursing organization. The eighty-eight thousand NPs practicing in 2000 represented an increase of twenty-four thousand over the number practicing in 1996. About 62 percent had completed a master's program and 6.5 percent had attended a post-RN certificate program. The vast majority—estimated at 90 percent—were employed in nursing, although not necessarily under the title of NP.

What They Do: Most NPs work in clinics, nursing homes, hospitals, or their own offices and have a specialty, for example, adult, family, or pediatrics. In an estimated twenty-one states they may prescribe medications. Many work as independent practitioners and can be reimbursed by Medicare or Medicaid for services rendered; others work for hospitals, HMOs, or private industry.

Earnings: The average salary for NPs in 1999 was $66,800, although earnings will depend to a large extent on where you work. NPs working in hospitals reported earning a maximum of $68,000 and a minimum of $65,000; those working for medical schools reported high salaries of $63,000 and low salaries of $60,000, according to the University of Texas Medical Branch at Galveston.

Certified Nurse-Midwife (CNM)

Number: There were approximately ninety-three hundred CNMs practicing in 2000, compared to sixty-five hundred in 1996.

Education: CNMs average about one and a half years of specialized education over and above nursing school, in thirty-nine accredited certificate programs or, like NPs, increasingly at the master's level.

What They Do: This advanced practice nursing specialty dates back to the early 1920s to Mary Breckenridge, a pioneering nurse who founded the Frontier Nursing Service (FNS) to provide family health services to isolated areas in the Appalachians by sending public health nurses to their patients by horseback. In 1929 she brought British nurse-midwives to the FNS. They were the first nurse-midwives in America. From these humble beginnings, the profession has grown considerably.

Today CNMs provide well-woman gynecological and low-risk obstetrical care including prenatal (prebirth), labor and delivery, and postdelivery care. According to a recent survey of the American College of Nurse Midwives, almost 95 percent of the births attended by CNMs were in hospitals, which also is where many CNMs (23.2 percent) are employed. They also work in birthing centers, homes, health maintenance organizations (HMOs), public health departments, private practices, and clinics.

Recent surveys by the American Nurses Association show that nurse-midwives performed fewer fetal monitors, episiotomies, and forced deliveries; administered fewer IVs; and delivered fewer low-birth-weight and premature infants. CNMs can prescribe medicine in twenty-one states.

Earnings: Salaries ranged from $65,000 to $75,000 in 1999, according to the American College of Nurse-Midwives.

Clinical Nurse Specialist (CNS)

Number: The number of clinical nurse specialists increased a little from 53,500 in 1996 to 54,000 in 2000.

Education: These are registered nurses with advanced nursing degrees—either master's or doctoral—who specialize in an area of practice such as mental health, gerontology, cardiac or cancer care, and community and neonatal health.

What They Do: CNSs work in many settings including hospitals, clinics, nursing homes, their own offices, and in other community settings such as industry, home care, and HMOs.

They are qualified to handle many physical and mental health problems, including primary care and psychotherapy. Typically CNSs conduct patient evaluations through screenings, tests, and their own observations; make diagnoses; and prescribe treatment. In addition to delivering direct patient care, they work in consultation, research, education, and administration. Some work in private practice and are eligible for direct reimbursement by Medicare, Medicaid, CHAMPUS, and private insurers.

Earnings: Depending on experience and setting, salaries for CNSs in 1998 ranged from about $43,000 to $48,000.

Certified Registered Nurse Anesthetist (CRNA)

Number: There were about twenty-nine thousand CRNAs practicing in 2000 compared to thirty thousand in 1996.

Education: CRNAs are registered nurses who have two to three years of education over and above the required four-year bachelor's degree, as well as national certification and recertification requirements.

What They Do: CRNAs administer more than 65 percent of all anesthetics given to patients every year in this, the oldest, of the advanced nursing specialties. They are also the sole providers of anesthetics in an estimated 85 percent of rural hospitals.

Working sometimes with an anesthesiologist, but often independently, these nurse specialists are employed in almost all settings where anesthetics are given: operating rooms, dentists' offices, outpatient surgery settings, birthing centers, and emergency centers.

Earnings: The average salary for CRNAs in 1998 was $82,000, with CRNAs working in hospitals earning the most and those in medical schools the least.

A Closer Look at Some Advanced Practice Nurses

To get a better idea of what advanced practice nurses do, let's take a look at some typical practitioners:

Marilyn Stokely, NP, works with a certified nurse-midwife out of a converted two-flat in East St. Louis, Illinois, which is almost completely lacking in medical care and where there is a critical shortage of physicians.

"It feels wonderful to make clinical decisions," she says. "I teach often, as well. For the most part, it's autonomous work. I can do physical exams, diagnose, and recommend nonprescription drugs."

In Illinois, NPs work together with physicians, whereas in four states they are able to set up their own offices. Because of state law, Stokely must depend on the physician who works with her to call in prescriptions she writes to a pharmacy. But NPs in more than twenty-one other states can write prescriptions without a physician.

Stokely, like many of her NP colleagues, emphasizes patient self-help and preventive medicine. She tells her patients to use the health care system properly by visiting her at a cost ranging from $5 to $50, rather than making an emergency room visit that could run several hundreds of dollars.

Nurse-midwife Mary Lu Dimond says that nurses spend more time explaining care and preventive health measures to patients than do doctors. She cited a study that showed that the typical advanced practice nurse spends half an hour with patients, compared with a five-minute doctor-patient encounter.

As one of her patients put it: "Nurse-midwives always encourage me to participate in my own education about pregnancy. When I had a question about some term or other, they even gave me textbooks to look at." During her third pregnancy, which some doctors termed high risk because she had almost had a miscarriage, this patient said the doctors looked "startled and annoyed" when she asked tough questions. "They provided excellent technical care, but seemed to lose interest when it came to educating me." Late in her pregnancy she switched to Nurse-Midwife Dimond and was much happier with her care.

The basic difference between nurse practitioners and physician assistants is one of approach. Nurse practitioners emphasize counseling, self-help, and preventive medicine. Their emphasis is on care and treatment *before* the patient develops a medical problem. Physician assistants, who work with their supervising physician, are more involved in care and treatment of patients who have already developed medical problems, but this, too, will vary. For instance, a PA who works in a Health Maintenance Organization (HMO) is more likely to emphasize preventive health care measures than one who works in a private setting or hospital.

For more information about advanced practice nursing, see *Opportunities in Nursing Careers* by Keville Frederickson and *Opportunities in Paramedical Careers* by Alex Kacen, both published by VGM Career Books.

6

Talks with Some PA Students

In this chapter you will find summaries of conversations with students in PA programs. These profiles will give you more of the flavor of what is involved in preparing for a career as a physician assistant.

Students at a Hospital-Based Program

Student 1

My major is in engineering and I have an associate degree from a local community college in fire science. I am married and have three kids—one, five, and seven. I was premed at Loyola University and have been serving as a paramedic on and off since 1975.

I wanted to leave the paramedic program and become a nurse, but then a friend, who happened to be a nurse, told me about the physician assistant program. I learned that after two years of study I could become a PA and could do much more than a nurse could.

So I applied to several schools, was accepted in a program in Illinois, and started last July. I expected it to be rough and, yes, it's about what I expected. It's a self-taught program to a great extent. You get books and attend lectures, but you have to pick up a lot of knowledge on your own. You must have a good background in medicine and in health care to understand the terminology.

I took anatomy, physiology, and microbiology at the community college before I was accepted here because they were prerequisites. But if I had a choice, I would have waited another year and taken a biology course and perhaps a pharmacology course.

I feel lucky to have been accepted here since it's among the least expensive of all the PA programs and offers an associate degree. To get into the bachelor's degree program, you have to have a stronger basic science background with some zoology and perhaps a lot of chemistry, both organic and inorganic.

Because our program is an associate degree program, there is not much offered in the way of financial aid, and that is a problem. If this were a bachelor's degree program and a four-year school, our financial aid office could do more and offer more financial support. So I have to work full-time, about thirty hours a week, while I go to school. I work several shifts a week at night, through a private company that contracts with local suburban fire departments.

Our curriculum here is excellent. We take a variety of courses and we are located in a large medical center with doctors and nurses, which helps a lot. We are in a real teaching environment here.

As it turns out, most of us in the program are studying for a second career, and our age group is from twenty-eight to thirty-five—quite a mature group. A lot of us have families and mortgages to pay on our homes.

Student 2

I am a first-year student and have a bachelor's degree from Marycrest College in Davenport, Iowa. I am twenty-nine years old and have been employed as a traveling nurse for the past five years.

As such I am able to go anywhere in the United States. My employer supplied traveling nurses and had contracts with hospitals all over the country. I worked in my hometown as a nurse for a year before joining my present company.

I had heard about the PA program about a year ago, although I had no personal contacts with anyone in the field. But I was looking for a change, and this seemed to be an excellent option.

The job sounded a lot like the nurse practitioner, which was another option I was considering. Both jobs allowed me to remain in a hospital setting, which I wanted. But I also wanted to do something a little different, something that offered more responsibility.

The curriculum at our school is challenging. I have had a lot of courses. For instance, as a critical care nurse, I studied physical assessment, just as we do in PA school. A lot of the work I have some background in, so it has not been that rough for me—yet.

Once I start my second year, with clinical rotations, and start doing procedures that I may not have done before, it will be rougher. For example, I have helped put in stitches, but I've never actually done them myself. A lot of basic knowledge I already have, but in PA school we go just a little beyond what I have been taught.

Ultimately, I would like to work as a member of a house staff in the critical care area. By that I am referring to departments in the hospital such as coronary care, intensive care, transplants, etc. I would, however, still like to work as a traveling PA.

As for financial aid, when I got my financial aid packet from school, I knew I would not be eligible for anything but a student loan, and later I learned that I would not even be eligible for that. Fortunately, I had enough money set aside to pay for tuition, books, and so forth, but even so I have had to work part-time, about twelve hours a week, usually on Sunday.

Through my work as a PA, I would like to have exposure to other fields of medicine besides critical care, such as working with children or pregnant women. This will help expand my knowledge of medicine, and I might find that I am interested in some other areas.

In this field you must be pretty flexible. My original intention was to work either in a rural area or in an inner city area in family practice. But in recent years, the field has expanded a lot to include surgery and critical care. It is a very broad field and allows you a lot of flexibility as to where you would like to hang your hat, so to speak, depending on your likes and dislikes and the need for your services.

If you would like to work in health care but are not quite sure of where, a job as a PA is an excellent choice because you can do so many different things and you're not stuck in any particular area of medicine. You might, for instance, be working in family practice and then decide that you would like to do surgery. As a PA, with some additional courses and experience, you could make the switch without too much trouble.

Student 3

I am twenty-seven and a second-year student from Chicago. I was a premed student at Northwestern University and was involved in

CHAMPS (Chicago-area health medical career programs) at the Illinois Institute of Technology.

While in college, I worked at a large hospital as a coagulating lab technician. I did two years of clinical work and two years of research. After graduating I decided that I was not ready to make the investment required, in terms of both time and money, in a medical education. So, the doctor I worked for hired me to work in his office at another suburban hospital, and I worked there for three years.

I was ready to go into some health care career, but it was not going to be medicine, that was certain. My entire life I had prepared myself for a medical career, but I was stymied by the length of time it took to qualify and the money involved. Instead, I went to CHAMPS and spoke with my counselor, who recommended that I talk with someone here at the PA school.

Prior to that I had never heard of the PA program. I spoke to the school's director and became interested in going for a master's degree, since I already had my bachelor's in psychology.

After this, I decided other programs would be too expensive to consider, plus I would have to pay an out-of-state fee. Knowing how hard it was to get into my school, I felt really good when I learned that I had been accepted.

At the time, I applied for the National Health Service Corps Scholarship, and I was lucky enough to get one. In my class three of us applied, but only two of us got this scholarship. It pays for two years of tuition, plus books and fees, and provides a monthly stipend of $769, less taxes. In return, I will give them two years of service, so when I graduate I will be working at a site that they consider is underserved—either rural or inner city. After I finish my National Health Service obligation, I most likely will work in the area of family practice or internal medicine.

The first year was pretty intense. I felt like we had to absorb a lot of information so that we could function in place of the physicians who would be leaving us in charge. That, at times, was overwhelming. But after I got into my second year, I was able to apply what I had learned and could see where it was worth all of the effort.

I see the role of a physician assistant as being the mid-level health provider who is needed so that all citizens can receive health care.

Students in a Medical Center–Based Program

Student 1

I am married and have two children and came here with my husband two years ago. He works for the Army Corps of Engineers. I am twenty-nine and from Tucson, Arizona, and I have a long and varied background in medicine. My interest in medicine developed while in high school. I started working in a doctor's office, and did this on and off for six years for two different doctors.

From there I started working on a degree in psychology. To get some experience in this area, I worked in an inpatient psychiatric unit, thirty-four beds, for adolescents and adults as a unit clerk for about a year.

Then I went to Iowa to help my mom, who has a chronic illness. I worked at the University of Iowa hospital and clinics for about a year as a nurse's aide on their medical-surgical floor. They had a pretty intensive training program, and we were allowed to do a lot of patient care.

When I returned to Tucson, I worked for a hospice for three years as a home health aide. Then I got a job as a supervisor of patient registration in a university medical center emergency room. I did that for a couple of years, got married, and came here.

During the years that I worked in internal medicine as a receptionist, I had heard of the PA program. One of the doctors had a PA working in the office. At the time I was premed, but it was really tough because I had to work to put myself through school and I still had to take care of my mom.

I figured I had a lot of background, so I started looking into PA programs and read about this one as well as a couple of others. I thought about going into the epidemiology-biostatistics field at the University of Illinois, but decided against it because epidemiology is entirely research-based and does not involve any contact with patients. The program here offered a very good clinical exposure, and since I had all of my basic science as well as eight or nine years of clinical experience, I was accepted.

What's unique about being a PA is that if everything does not work out quite as you anticipated, you have the opportunity to switch into some other area of medicine. Working as a PA also offers two main benefits: the chance to earn a good salary, and the opportunity to work with patients in a meaningful one-on-one basis, where you are entirely involved in their health care from the very first day.

Right now I am in my clinical rotations and am starting with obstetrics/gynecology. I have done a lot of other rotations, including pediatrics at an HMO in the city and psychiatry at the osteopathic hospital. After I finish school, we plan to move back to the Southwest. We'll probably live in Albuquerque, and I'd like to work in some area of public health, maybe in the Indian Health Service.

You have to be very highly motivated to succeed in this profession. The PA program is very intensive. You are learning in two years what it takes a physician basically four years to learn, and you must be able to organize your time to take all of this in. If you are good at getting your resources, you'll do well. But you must be self-directed and able to resolve any doubts you may have had about not being able to get into medical school.

For me this was never much of a consideration. I wanted to do primary medical care and that's what the PA is trained to do. Of course, many PAs branch out into the various specialties, and that's okay, too. Basically, I guess what it takes is the ability to work with all kinds of people and to accept them for who they are.

For me, at age twenty-nine, becoming a PA was attractive. Not only can I work part-time or half-time, but I can switch fields if I am interested in doing something else.

Student 2

I will be sixty-two years old in June. I have never gone to college. I am married and have three daughters and five grandchildren. I had been in finance and retailing for about thirty years but wanted to get into something more rewarding. When I was offered the chance to give a couple of lectures on business at the community college, I picked up brochures on other courses that were offered, and that's how I got into the emergency medical technician program. I took that program and the paramedical program at a local hospital for nine months. Finally, I went through pediatric life support and trauma training. I went back to school, became a paramedic, and worked at that for about seven years.

After a while though, that too seemed to lose its kick. I read a notice on the bulletin board at the fire department about the PA program. It sounded good, so I called the school, filled out an application, and enrolled. I took the prerequisites for the program—physiology, anatomy, and microbiology—and courses in genetics at a local college.

Here the first year's study is primarily self-learning. I must have put in about five to six hours of study a day in addition to class work. I am now in the second year and going through clinical rotations prior to finishing this August. I also still work part-time with the fire department and am on call with them for weekend duty if they need me.

Taking part in the rotations has been just great. They are informative and I have learned a lot more than I ever realized I would. We have been taught how to do physicals and how to take case histories, and that's 70 percent of what goes into making a diagnosis. From that point, I know what resources are available and I can look up the information that I need. In the rotations, you begin to experience what you learned in your first year on how the basic sciences fit together. But it's a very concentrated program and it might be better to spread it out over three years. There is so much to learn.

The patients seem to like us very much and treat us as though we were their doctors. It's that simple, because we diagnose, treat, and follow-up on them. But we can't prescribe medications here in Illinois; we have to get the supervising physicians to do this for us.

After school, I would like to give something back to society. I would like to work in the Indian Health Service helping those who are underserved. I may go into trauma or emergency medicine and would like to teach a little, too. I am also thinking of taking physiology, which is being offered as part of the master's program.

The biggest problem that we have as PAs is that many people have no real understanding of what we are and what we do. Doctors' attitudes are getting better and on the whole they seem to be receptive, although a few are still hostile. But we have good acceptance from the medical students. My classmates and I have worked alongside medical students for each of the rotations, and we have been accepted both by the students and the doctors as part of the team.

As to the PA program itself, to do well you have to be totally immersed in it. There is not a moment when I am not involved with this program one way or the other. I have to drive to school about an hour and a half every day. I have not listened to the radio in the nearly two years that I have been in the program. What I do listen to is tapes on medicine. I must have twenty tapes in the car on pediatrics alone, and that is just fine because one of the ways that you learn is through repetition. There are no geniuses in this field who after one run-through on a tape can say that they know it all. Most students have a very positive attitude, but if you enter the program with an arrogant attitude, you won't do well.

Most of the students here receive scholarships, and even if they don't have any financial aid, this school is not so expensive compared to many others.

The term *physician assistant* is somewhat misleading in that a lot of people confuse us with medical assistants and think that we are the people who get physicians their coffee, run their errands, etc. They would be amazed at what we are able to do to assist the doctors and the patients. I have just come off a pediatrics rotation where I cared for fifteen to twenty kids a day. I would review what

I had done and seen with my doctor after each day's work. And you know what he told me? "Keep doing your thing. You won't need me."

Even though doctors have several years of medical school plus two or three years of residency and a year of internship on us, I would still like to challenge them in the national board examination. I think I would do just as well. I might need a little more time to study, but I sure would like to have the opportunity to see what I could do. I think that everybody would be surprised. Our standards for study are very high.

7

CONVERSATIONS WITH PROFESSIONALS

IN THE LAST chapter we learned about how some students, with varying backgrounds and lives, found out about and decided to pursue the rigorous and demanding education program required to become PAs. In this chapter we'll take a look at how certified PAs working in diverse situations handle the day-to-day demands their profession makes on them.

PA with a Family Practice

I work in a suburban area north of the city with a group of eight other physicians all specializing in family practice. I was the first PA hired to work in this practice. This came about because one of the physicians was planning to retire and the other physicians wanted someone to help take over his patient load. But they didn't know if they wanted to bring in another physician or a PA, so they researched it, decided to try a PA, and here I am.

In rural areas there is a trend to hire PAs to help doctors handle their loads and to spread the duties, so to speak. This is why the profession came into being in the first place—to go into areas where there were shortages of physicians and help out. Now we are working in every area in medicine and in every locality of the country—metropolitan as well as small communities. There was even a PA in the White House during the Reagan administration. Our current president is very much for mid-level providers, which is what we are, and I don't see him changing his mind in the future.

When I was hired, the doctors in the group agreed that this would be a good step. The only question was whether patients would let me treat them once they learned I was a PA and not a physician. Since none of us had any experience with this situation, we were all uptight about it. But even during the first month on the job, I think I had convinced everyone—both patients and doctors alike—of my competence, and there has not been any problem ever since.

In general I love my work and would not want to do anything different. Typically, the student coming out of medical school is about $100,000 in debt, at the very least; my debt coming out of PA school was about $12,000, which is bad enough, but not nearly as bad as the financial load that medical students carry. Fortunately, financial aid is available through your school and should cover most of your costs.

One thing I don't like is not having the power to write prescriptions in this state. Although it does not hamper us from getting needed prescriptions for patients, it can sometimes be a problem. And the need for a doctor who lives forty or fifty miles away to come in once a week to sign papers is a real hassle. We can manage all right, but it is something of a pain.

Currently, I do professional placement of students for the state, and we have about forty jobs that are open to qualified PAs. At the moment we have job offers for just about all students even before they are finished with their training. We're not turning out nearly enough graduates to meet the job opportunities. Nationally there are six to eight jobs per PA.

I am also on the teaching staff of a PA program in the area and we allow for first-year students to watch a PA at work in the real world. This really helps to motivate students.

Right now all PAs must be certified to practice or to use the title "PA-C." We also are required to carry one hundred hours of CME (continuing medical education) credit every two years after we finish school. And we have to be recertified every six years. This is unique to our profession, which should help to address the concerns of those who may be critical of our training.

PA in Endocrinology

I graduated from the PA program in 1990 and have been practicing now for about twelve years. I attended Alderson-Broaddus College in Philippi, West Virginia, because at that time there were no PA programs in this area. The first was started here about six years ago, and now two more are underway—one in connection with a medical school and the other at a college of osteopathy.

I came to the PA program as part of a career exploration course that I took in high school. We looked into various careers and I decided to research one on the PA profession after I read about it in a magazine. I wrote to the American Academy of Physician Assistants, and they sent me material for my paper.

I had wanted to do something in medicine before that. I knew I didn't want to be a nurse, but all the years of study and residency involved in qualifying to become a doctor seemed too long. So the PA program was a sort of a compromise. Medicine, with its fellowships and residencies that you had to complete before you could specialize, well, it felt like you would be studying for half of your life. The PA approach sounded like a perfect opportunity to do most of the things that physicians do, without having to complete all of those years of study. I think of PA school as a crash course in medicine. Most PA programs are two years in length, but you have to have either a bachelor's degree or at least two years of college.

My first job as a PA was working in a northern suburb for an internist. Later I worked at the local county jail and a now defunct hospital in the city. Then I accepted an assignment as an administrator for a health care unit at the local federal corrections center and also worked at a family practice clinic in the inner city for several years.

In the latter practice, I had my own list of appointments, which were all my own patients. They would come in specifically to see me. However, if I had a question about anything or if I came across something out of the ordinary or abnormal, I would contact my supervising physician to help me decide how to handle the situation.

When you come out of PA school, you're like a family practice doctor. You're trained in primary care medicine and go through the various rotations in surgery, medicine, obstetrics-gynecology, and pediatrics, but basically you are a family practitioner, just like a medical school graduate would be before he or she completes a residency to become a specialist. The same holds true of the PA program. You go to postgraduate training to specialize in certain phases of medicine, or you learn on the job by working for a specialist.

Nurse practitioners function pretty much the same as we do. It's the training that's different. NPs are nurses first; they train as nurses and then go on to some additional school for NP designation. The time required to complete the program may vary from one school to the other. It's not as standardized as ours is—two years for PA school after two years of undergraduate college.

Our training is always geared to competency as a mid-level practitioner, but I have worked at places where there were NPs doing essentially the same thing I did. The duties of PAs are pretty similar to those of NPs. They may, for instance, screen kids that come in with some health complaint and decide on appropriate tests required—a blood count, a chest X ray, or whatever.

I like to think of the PA as someone who is helping to solve health care problems in this country by working in medically underserved areas—just like when I worked in the ghetto and in prison settings. It is hard getting physicians to go into those places, just like it is hard to get physicians to go into sparsely settled areas, like Wyoming, for instance, where the closest doctor might be a hundred miles away.

The other area of employment is working for physicians who are too busy to handle everything themselves but who don't want to work with another doctor as a partner. If you had another physician working with you, you would have to give up some of your power in running the practice, and it may be hard to get agreement on many matters. So, many physicians who have growing practices and want to maintain better control look to the PA as the answer to this problem. The PA is their employee, accountable to them and under their supervision, and they will do things the way the physician wants them to.

Although a relatively new profession, studies have shown that patient acceptance of PAs is just great because PAs spend more time with patients, have a nice bedside manner, and take the time to explain a given test or treatment. Also, most physicians who have worked with PAs have no problem accepting them. The problems occur with doctors who are ignorant of what PAs do and of their competence.

At first I was fearful about patients not accepting me in my current job as an assistant to an endocrinologist. Previously I had worked in an inner city clinic where I was really needed and the patients could have cared less if I was a doctor or a PA. But this turned out to be a needless fear since the physician I work for is very busy, and I have much more time to work with patients and help allay their fears.

Here in Illinois we have to work with our supervising physician in prescribing medications, but in most other states PAs have the authority to prescribe.

To know if the field is right for you, I believe you must first have a strong interest in medicine, a good background in science, and you should be able to see yourself as a physician. But you may have limited resources, and your grade point average may not be high enough to get into medical school. So, if you aspire to medicine, but have financial or educational limitations, you might want to consider becoming a PA. Also, while you are in high school, you could get a job either as a candy striper or as an orderly in a local hospital. You would then have a good idea of what the work is like.

I remember that as part of my PA training I had to work in a pediatrics ward in a hospital. We had a little boy come into the emergency room with what we thought was a drug overdose because he was acting so lethargic. He was in the ward about an hour when he died of what turned out to be a massive aneurysm, a weakened blood artery that burst in his brain. I decided there and then that I could not work in this area of medicine. Fortunately, there are many other areas of medicine that you can go into if one particular area is not right for you.

I have seen many medical students who have the brains and are doing well in school, but who have absolutely no idea of what medicine is like in the hospital or in rural areas. They may get an A in chemistry now, but when they go into the emergency room or see their first patient with a gunshot or stab wound, they may faint.

As to the future of this career, this is definitely an expanding field. Only a year or two ago in the listing of careers to go into, the *Wall Street Journal* showed PA among the top five careers for high school students.

PA Certified in Surgery and Vascular Surgery

When I started in 1976 the profession was almost unknown. The idea of establishing such a profession originated in the mid-60s, but in 1976 hardly anyone knew anything about the field or what PAs were supposed to be doing. There was no local school and we had none in the state until 1987.

One of my associates had gone into a kind of nurse practitioner program, but it wasn't called that at the time. She alerted me to the fact that the PA program was having a qualifying exam. But that wasn't enough to be allowed to practice in Illinois as a PA. You still had to pass the boards to be licensed. So I couldn't be licensed until after I had finished my preceptorship training. So I completed my training and since then have been working in a job that I love.

Today you would have to go through two years of college and two years of PA school to qualify for the profession. Some programs are four years and combine PA training with two years of undergraduate work.

In our profession, you work with your supervising physician and help with what he or she does. I make rounds and I assist in surgery, just like residents. I am not a scrub nurse or a circulating nurse. In surgery, I function as a surgical PA. Most patients are unaware that the person assisting the physician can be either another doctor or a surgical assistant.

Surgical assistants suture patients, may retract, and do whatever is required to make the operation easier to perform. Some surgical assistants may open and close patients, for example, during cardiovascular surgery. We even assist in bypass surgery and may take veins from the legs to use as bypass veins.

As a PA, I do the history and the physical and often counsel patients. You do things that the doctor does—initiate orders for medication, tests, and so forth. In the hospital, the doctor must countersign your orders, usually within twenty-four or forty-eight hours. In actuality, you communicate with each other whenever necessary. When I am making rounds and seeing patients, I introduce myself as the PA, take a history, do the physical, and then look at the chart to see what has been done and what still needs to be done. If my supervising doctor is at another hospital, I can still check with him and get treatment underway. For patients who have undergone surgery, I write the postop orders and see the patients daily. Nothing is done unless there are written orders.

To join a hospital staff, you go through the same credentialing procedure that the MD does. I cannot assist at just any hospital, only the one where my supervising physician practices. My surgeon is on the staff of another hospital, but I am not on that one yet. They use residents at that hospital. In a way being a PA is like being a resident.

I recommend the profession without reservation if you are qualified and have the training. It is very gratifying to be able to see patients from the time they come in with a problem until they are discharged. Working in the operating room is also very satisfying, but you don't have the initial contact with the patient. You are limited to your work in surgery. But as a PA you get to see more—the entire problem and how it is resolved.

I wear my PA badge at all times when I am visiting patients either before or after surgery. As a PA I always make sure the patient knows that I am not a doctor, but many insist on calling me doctor anyhow. It is really a compliment to be placed in the same category as a physician, and it makes me feel good.

On the whole the patients are very accepting of PAs. Often they are afraid to ask their doctors questions, and they feel more comfortable talking with someone who works for the doctor. Having someone who can explain conditions and procedures and answer any questions really improves the quality of care that patients receive.

I believe that in the future there will be even more opportunities for PAs because we are providing a service for both the patient and the doctor. In many small towns, the only practitioner may be a PA. And in the city, we help take a lot of the load off doctors' shoulders.

In the hospital, we can write orders for medication and treatment, but in the office, PAs don't have prescriptive powers in Illinois. We have to have the doctor sign the prescription or call in the order and leave it with the pharmacist. We can write prescriptions in forty-six states now. But even among the states that do allow PAs prescriptive authority there are different rules on what they can or cannot prescribe.

Even though we are dependent practitioners in the sense that we are supervised, PAs still have to be independent and self-reliant because we may not be able to have much contact with either other PAs or doctors.

I feel more comfortable working as a surgeon assistant. That's where I believe I can contribute the most for my patients. And in this profession, you can always change your job. Each new post is a challenge. Nothing is exactly the same. If you switch from working for one surgeon to another, there would be a lot of changes to get used to because no two surgeons work exactly alike. You have to be willing to learn and must be flexible and open-minded.

As to my hours, although they are not quite as long as a surgeon's, I still work a lot—probably about sixty hours or so a week. But we get additional salary for working a longer workweek, as well as other benefits. My supervising surgeon works seven days a week because he makes rounds on Sunday as well as during the rest of the week.

But it's really important that you like the work. If you don't, then you definitely should not get into it. Working in a hospital as a nurse's aide or as a volunteer or possibly even in a doctor's office as a receptionist, will give you some idea of how things are done in a hospital.

Most of the people coming into the profession today do not have any specific experience in medicine or nursing. But you should be aware that some of the programs do require that you have some sort of background in health care.

I feel that it's very important for the profession that we have one hundred hours of continuing medical education every two years because you are always learning while you are working. When a person comes in for a simple hernia repair, you need to find out if he or she has diabetes or some other cardiovascular problems that you should be aware of because this can affect the treatment that you give them. You don't just treat the hernia but the whole person, taking into account their total health picture before deciding on the appropriate treatment.

PA Practicing in Obstetrics/Gynecology

I work in a small community of about forty-five thousand in northwestern Illinois about fifty miles from where I live. I was a premed student at the University of Iowa, where I received my bachelor's degree in 1973, and then I enrolled in the PA program at the University of Iowa College of Medicine.

I could have enrolled a year earlier but decided to wait. I wanted to go into medicine, but I looked into the PA program because I had several children and only wanted to work part-time. The PA field offers the same challenges of medicine but without having to work weekends or nights or being on call. My husband earns a good salary, so for me it isn't a matter of needing the money.

When I first started as a PA, I worked on a part-time basis for an obstetrician-gynecologist, and this was followed by a stint of eight years in family practice, also part-time. I still work part-time, two full days a week and two half days.

I was the first PA in the community, so it took a while for me to earn the respect of the patients, doctors, and staff. But today, nearly everyone in the community knows what a PA is, and we now have three PAs who are working in the area of industrial medicine.

The choice of doctors that you work for is very important. It's like a marriage, and you must take care to make the right choice. I have always been fortunate in my choice of doctors and have always had a good relationship with my supervising physician. But sometimes the doctors may think of the PA as a doormat to walk on.

I work in an office with two doctors, one of whom is my supervising physician. I do almost everything that an obstetrician or gynecologist would do, including colposcopy, which is an evaluation of an abnormal Pap smear as seen through a scope, and insertion of intrauterine devices (IUDs) to prevent pregnancy. I also assist in surgery.

I wanted to be in some phase of medicine ever since I was an eighth grader. I worked as a nurse's aide in a hospital and also did volunteer work while I was in high school. It is important that you are involved in some phase of health care work while you are in high school, so that you can determine your aptitude for the work and your ability to help people who are sick. Also, you should have a good background in science and math and you should like people since you will be working with all sorts of patients, many of them not at their best.

Another PA in Family Practice

I work as a PA in a small family practice in a rural area in south central Illinois. After finishing the premed program at Millikin

University in Decatur, I completed my RN training at Decatur Memorial Hospital School of Nursing and was thinking of going into medicine. But after working as a nurse for seven years, I found that I was considered too old to do this, and the fact that I was a female did not help. So, I was not encouraged to continue in medicine.

Then I noticed in a medical journal an opportunity for a four-year preceptorship, after which I would be able to take the boards and be licensed as a PA. So that's what I did, and I continued with the same doctor for nearly twenty-six years until he died. I then got my current job with another family practitioner, where among other duties I assist in surgery and work in a clinic in a community of forty-eight hundred people. I like the work very much and have a good opportunity to apply what I learned in my training.

I love my job and enjoy working in a small community where I have more personal contact with my patients and get to know them better.

Director of a PA Program at an Osteopathic Medical School

Our program was established about four years ago when the osteopathic college decided to begin a college of allied health and started looking at a program that filled a community need. It was determined that the physician assistant program was a profession that needed more practitioners and offered excellent prospects for success, since there was only one other program in the entire metropolitan area.

One class has currently matriculated and our sixteen students are beginning their clinical rotations as part of their second-year program. I have been involved with the program as a consultant since 1990 and was appointed director in February 1993.

Our new class consists of forty students, and we are increasing our capacity to fifty students starting in June. Of these, thirty-four are from out of state. The class is about 56 percent male and 44 percent female.

If a student comes to us with some health care experience, they'll get credit for that. It demonstrates their dedication to health care and their personal commitment and ability to relate as a professional on a personal level. But we require that applicants have completed sixty semester hours of college or ninety quarter hours (the equivalent of two years of college) and have a C or better in all courses.

When we receive the students' applications, we look over their records. Even if some fall short of specific requirements, their academic records may be so good that we will consider accepting them. If they meet the academic requirements, they are invited for an interview with a screening committee that consists of three faculty members.

Their recordation goes to the full admissions committee who will then look over the records, taking into account the interviewers' comments and evaluations, and either accept them, put them on hold, or reject them.

The PA profession involves a variety of skills and experience of the people who are in it. For many it is their second or third career. In our present class, for instance, we have a former pharmacist, an executive, a nurse, three former emergency technicians (paramedics), and a former researcher in anatomy.

In the first year of the program, students take such courses as human anatomy, biochemistry, and behavioral medicine, and in the fall quarter they will take other courses such as physiology, emergency medicine, epidemiology, and clinical diagnosis. The load is pretty heavy—fifteen to seventeen hours per quarter.

In the second year our students begin clinical rotations: emergency medicine for four weeks, family medicine for ten weeks, geriatric medicine for two weeks, internal medicine for four weeks, and obstetrics/gynecology for four weeks. Rotations are held both inside and outside of the hospital.

Our tuition now is $9,000 a year for in-state students and $10,500 for those from out of state. Most students do have loans, however, to help defray the costs—some federal loans and some from local banks. The tuition covers attendance for four quarters a year—the year round. Most of our students will probably be carrying a debt of $25,000 when they finish, but after graduation they will be able to earn from $40,000 to $45,000 per year on entry-level jobs.

Students cannot work while they are in the program. During their first year they may be able to pick up some money by babysitting, tutoring, and so forth, but they cannot work full-time. In the second year, students are on call and must be in the clinics. Their hours are erratic, and there is no way they can work a job on a regular basis.

Some classes are held together with medical students. When they first come here, PAs take an anatomy course specifically designed for them. Other courses such as pharmacology they take with medical and pharmacology students as well. They also take pathology with medical students. Incidentally, our students do pretty well gradewise—they are about in the middle. We figure that on the average for each of the sixteen hours of course work that they take per quarter, they will have to study an additional three hours, for a total of forty-eight hours of study a week per quarter.

If they can get through the first year of school, the chances are pretty good that they will make it. In my experience, there are a few individuals who won't do well in the clinical areas. They may have the book knowledge, but when it comes to actually dealing with patients or doctors, they fall short. During the first year we watch them closely in such courses as therapeutic skills, clinical medicine, and clinical diagnosis, which are all designed to see how well the students can do with patients. This way they are exposed to both physicians and patients from the start.

Our PA courses help us determine how well students will function in the clinical area. Some with a short fuse won't make it, or they may not know how to handle themselves with patients or how to talk to physicians. In these cases, we hold the students back until they can show that they can handle the work.

All PA programs have excellent chances for success because of the tremendous need for PAs, and our community is becoming increasingly knowledgeable and accepting of PAs. There are currently about six to eight jobs for every PA coming out of school. It's almost impossible to find enough graduates with the educational and licensure qualifications to do the work. They are very much in short supply.

Our students take the national boards for PA and do as well as other PA students. Once they pass their national boards, they must apply for licensing and can then practice as PAs. In addition, once they pass the boards for certification, they must be recertified every six years, and every two years PAs must submit evidence of having completed one hundred hours of continuing medical education.

You as a student must evaluate the intrinsic value of being a PA. You must decide in high school if you want to be in a helping profession and if so, which direction to go in. There are those who feel they want to be in charge of the process. They want total control. Such individuals need to go on to medical school, and we encourage them to do so. But that is a long row to go, involving at least eleven years of study, up to fifteen years and even more in certain cases.

If, on the other hand, you can accept the fact that your role in medicine will always be a part of the physician's practice, and that the physician will always have the final word, then you should definitely consider being a PA. Then you have the opportunity to make a difference in this world—to help the human condition.

I was one of the first to take the national boards. This profession has allowed me to do things in addition to providing patient care. I am also involved in the delivery of health care in the community as a whole, working on the education and health policies of various committees.

In my own case I never aspired to practicing medicine. I was a corpsman in the air force, did a lot of independent duty, and was fortunate to come out at a time when a lot of military people were going right into PA school. I didn't want to have the demands on my life and time that a physician encounters. Now my spare time is my own, and I can do the things that I want to.

The physician must train for many years to reach a specialty level of competence, and once there, he or she cannot easily change directions. But as a PA you have alternatives and options. You can work in surgery, and if that doesn't suit you, switch to family practice, obstetrics/gynecology, or whatever. There is a lot of latitude in the profession that allows for change.

As a PA coming out of school you can work in surgery, but if you have been working in primary care and want to switch after several years, you might want to go to postgraduate school for additional experience in surgery or whatever. You have the basic foundation and can add whatever other courses you need through postgraduate work or through on-the-job experience.

Director of a Hospital-Based PA Program Affiliated with a Community College

After several years of planning, our program finally was begun when the dean at Citywide College of Chicago—our original director—accepted the first class. We were the only PA program in Illinois, and as such, the only publicly supported program in the state. Illinois had no official program until we started ours, but there were lots of jobs then just as there are now. Here at Cook County Hospital, the Department of Family Practice had for many years tried to fill their openings with PAs. The hospital has had PAs on the staff since 1976, and to be approved by the state, they had to prove need.

Our program is no longer affiliated with Citywide but with Malcolm X College, another of Chicago's city colleges, where most of the health programs are centralized. We send out more than a thousand applications a year, of which about two hundred are returned. From these we select seventy-five for interview. Of these, twenty-five are admitted per year. To date we have had sixty-two graduates.

Our students come from throughout the city and suburbs, from the northern Indiana area, and from downstate Illinois. The typical age of the students is thirty-four, considerably above the college level, and it's about fifty-fifty men and women, and thirty-five percent blacks and Hispanics. About half of the class have their bachelor's degrees; a few even have their master's degrees. We require that students have at least two years of college with course work in general sciences, humanities, and literature.

A lot of our students put aside the application process until they have completed the specific courses required as well as the work experience. Most of the two hundred applications that we receive yearly are from qualified students. We screen applicants for those with the best experience, the best academic record, and so forth.

Students should not be disappointed that they cannot be accepted right out of high school. They need a thorough grounding in the fundamentals of medicine and the basic sciences before they can be accepted in our program. They also need health care experience so that they have some knowledge of medicine and medical terminology, which will help them with their course work. In addition, students must have a minimum of a 2.0 grade point average (C average), but this is just the minimum, and they should have a higher grade point average to ensure acceptance in the program.

Students should realize that there are certificate programs, bachelor's programs, and now there are several master's programs, and the requirements for admission to each may vary quite a bit since the emphasis in each is different.

Because we are not a bachelor's degree program, we don't require prerequisites involving specialized sciences such as human biology, anatomy, and physiology. Chicago Osteopathic does, but we do not. We require only one chemistry course; Chicago Osteopathic requires considerably more in this area. And to illustrate how different schools go about selecting their students, Osteopathic might, for instance, take someone with a lot of chemistry and little experience, or perhaps just the opposite. We, however, insist that our students have at least some health care experience.

When students come here, they get an anatomy review course and some physiology and cadaver dissection. In the fall they start their medical courses, which are basically clinical medicine, including preventive medicine, epidemiology, cardiology, pulmonary medicine, and nephrology, and a lecture and discussion course. They also receive courses in physical assessment, which focuses on performing a complete physical exam; on principles of interviewing and taking a patient history; and on clinical skills, such as interpretations of lab tests, biochemistry, hematology, and urinalysis. We also require that students take a course in medical terminology and fundamentals of speech, which will be made a prerequisite in the near future. In addition, we are looking into the possibility of hooking up with a bachelor's degree program.

In the second semester, students are assigned to preceptors (practicing PAs) for ten-week stints, during which they see patients in the hospital. The preceptor might be an MD, a PA, or an RN. Students also learn how to interpret EKGs and X rays. Medical pharmacology is a very comprehensive program involving a lot of time and lectures.

The summer programs are very practical in nature: how to suture, how to put a limb into a cast, how to prepare for the operating room, how to gown, principles of asepsis (maintaining a germ-free environment), how to start an intravenous solution (IV), and how to do an injection or bladder catheterization.

Our classes run anywhere from 8:00 A.M. to 1:00 P.M., Monday through Saturday. By the end of the first year, students are in class from 9:00 A.M. to 5:00 P.M. The first summer they are in class 9:00 A.M. to 5:00 P.M. daily, studying principles of good nutrition, meeting the nutrition needs of the diabetic, or learning about a low-cholesterol or low-salt diet.

Over the course of the second year, students take eight clinical rotations, each for six weeks. Some of the students go to a medical center in Flint, Michigan, for this. Some may do a surgery rotation at the trauma unit at Cook County Hospital, or possibly the cardio-thoracic unit at Northwestern, or this can be an elective. Several students have already applied to work at the Federal Bureau of Prisons to fulfill this requirement. Pediatrics they do at Mt. Sinai Hospital, and this is a combination of inpatient and outpatient work. Obstetrics/gynecology is also such a combination, as is mental health and psychiatry. Internal Medicine I is predominantly an in-hospital setting. We think the students get a very good grounding in clinical medicine.

We are preparing first-year students for their second year and second-year students for graduation, board exams, and licensure. The two classes meet every six weeks or so for a few hours to discuss matters of importance to both.

Credit hours do not suggest actual study hours, not by a long shot, and students are expected to study at home or in the library. We try to pick students most likely to persevere in such an intensive program right up to the end.

If students are from the suburbs, they apply to their local community college for reimbursement of the difference between tuition for the suburbs and city residents. Once finished, our kids place themselves with the offers that seem most attractive, having received job offers throughout the year, some of them with the understanding that a job with a good employer awaits them.

We do have a bulletin board where job listings as they come in are posted for students to look at. We also help students prepare their résumés. Occasionally, employers will come for recruitment luncheons. There is no lack of job opportunities, and we have about six to eight openings per student.

As to where they go, about half of last year's class is working in primary care, for family practice, obstetrics/gynecology, pediatrics, and internal medicine doctors. The other half is working in surgery or in other specialties.

Many are employed by a hospital, or by a private practitioner, or by both. We're proud of the fact that about 20 percent of our students work either at Cook County Hospital or Cook County Jail.

As to financial aid, our accessibility to federal funds is limited and we have to spread out what little is available among all of our students. Aid is available through the National Service Corps scholarships, which three of our students are currently receiving. And we hope to be able to expand the program to cover additional students.

Also many, if not most of our students, have already received all of the financial aid to which they are entitled as undergraduates in other schools, so it is difficult for them to obtain additional funds. Most of them know this and begin to collect the funds they will need for PA school several years prior to their actual enrollment.

There are a few private scholarships available to PA students through several national organizations, but these are usually limited to about $1,000 each, which is not much when figured against the total cost of a PA education.

We advise our students not to work while they attend class. It is simply too intensive a program. Our studies show that students who attempt to work while in school suffer in their class work.

8

A LOOK AT THE FUTURE

As HAS BEEN mentioned many times in this book, the outlook for physician assistants is bright indeed. With six to eight openings for every PA graduate, how could it be anything else? And with an estimated five thousand new graduates joining the ranks of those already in practice, it looks like the supply will not be adequate to meet the demand. So you can afford to be choosy. You can decide where you want to practice, what kind of a practice you would like to be part of, and the type of setting that you would prefer, be it for the government, for industry, in a hospital or medical center, or in private practice.

True, several new schools are expected to open or are already functional, and that should increase the number of qualified PA graduates considerably. Even so, the number of openings per graduate is expected to remain largely the same. The reason? As the word about the competency of PAs continues to spread and more and more physicians learn about them, they will undoubtedly consider hiring more PAs. The reasons may be financial—to help cut costs in opening a practice—which can be a very important consideration in many areas, especially in rural areas where income is very limited. Or, as has already been noted, the physician or group may not wish to relinquish control of the practice to another physician as an associate or partner.

Consequently openings will continue to expand over the years. In fact, the Bureau of Labor Statistics has predicted a 48 percent growth in the profession over the next eight years, making physician assistant one of the fastest growing professions of all in the near future.

Some Important Considerations in Deciding on a PA Career

In addition to excellent job prospects, there are some other considerations that should be a part of your decision-making process. For one, working as a PA means that you give up a good deal of your autonomy. In many cases you cannot do what you want to; in fact, in all cases, your own ideas may have to take a back seat to those of your supervising physician, who is after all the boss. If your relationship with your supervising physician is more on the loose side, he or she may give you considerable leeway in arriving at important decisions; but even so, your decisions will always be subject to change. If you think you can subordinate your ideas to those of the supervising physician—great—then the PA profession may be ideal for you. If not, you might want to consider becoming a physician yourself.

Because of the unique relationship that governs your actions with those of your supervising physician, it is important that he or she respects your skills and has complete confidence in your abilities. If you do not have your supervisor's complete trust and respect, it can undermine your entire relationship with him or her.

Fortunately, the profession does offer a certain amount of flexibility, and if for any reason you should want to change the kind of practice you are associated with, you can usually do so without too much fuss. After all, you already have the necessary basic skills to do the job and can go on to expand your skills working in another area.

It's also very important to remember that the PA program is very intensive, involving nearly all of your time and energy for the entire two-year training period. Such a commitment can well affect your personal life and relationships with your spouse and children, to name but a few.

Finally, you should consider that the cost of a PA education is considerable, and unless you are independently wealthy or have acquired the necessary funds through earnings from previous jobs, you will be hard pressed to meet these costs. Even so, as has already been noted, funds are there to help finance your education, assuming that you have the brains and the prerequisite academic requirements.

As to the region in which job opportunities are the best, in a 1999 survey in *Medical Economics* of nonphysician personnel involved in health care, respondents said that the best practice opportunities were in the Great Lakes Region, while the worst were in the Southwest.

That same survey revealed that younger physicians were more likely to hire PAs than older ones. It further revealed that in the mind of the physician, the physician assistant and the nurse practitioner were basically on the same level as to skills and training. Finally, the survey indicated that orthopedic surgeons, ophthalmologists, and cardiovascular surgeons were more likely to favor PAs over NPs.

If you have taken all of these considerations into account and still believe the physician assistant career is for you, then by all means go for it, for it will almost certainly bring the respect, security, and financial and personal rewards that make a career worthwhile.

Where to Practice

What do the experts see as to where you will be working in the next few years? Although most PAs are expected to continue in primary care, there most likely will be a decrease in the percentage of PAs working in family practice. This will, however, be largely offset by an increasing number of PAs working in the other areas of primary care—internal medicine, pediatrics, and obstetrics/gynecology.

Then, too, as the number of women entering the field increases, you can expect to see a sharp growth in the number of PAs practicing in the areas of primary care that have had the greatest appeal for women—pediatrics and obstetrics/gynecology. At the same time a dramatic increase is seen in the number of PAs practicing as specialists—in surgery and its various offshoots, ophthalmology, urology, and so forth.

Also expected to change are the settings in which PAs practice:

PAs in Hospital-Based Settings: With hospitals facing declining patient populations and income, look for increased use of PAs to strengthen house staffs, reduce the number of residents in certain specialties, and provide outpatient and home care services as extensions of the hospital. Hospitals can enjoy substantial savings in salaries by hiring more PAs.

PAs in Office-Based Settings: With HMOs and PPOs (preferred provider organizations) serving as ever increasingly fertile grounds for employment of PAs, look to more and more PAs being added to HMO staffs. At the same time, there will be fewer jobs in rural and metropolitan areas as more and more family physicians are attracted to smaller communities or those with the greatest need.

PAs in Other Institutional Settings: Job opportunities in prisons, nursing homes, and mental health centers will grow, primarily because of the cost savings involved.

PAs in Other Patient Settings: Increasingly, PAs will begin to be employed in areas of occupational and industrial medicine, especially in health promotion and disease prevention. PAs also will be utilized to assist in alcohol and drug rehabilitation programs. As freestanding health facilities such as surgicenters and emergency centers continue to grow, there will be additional openings for PAs in these locations.

All of these areas can be expected to offer more opportunities for PAs even while openings for physicians as a whole decline. The reason? It is more cost effective to hire PAs even as health care facilities reduce the number of physicians they employ, especially specialists.

Will Health Care Be Compromised?

However, the question remains of whether health care institutions in hiring more PAs endanger quality of care. There is no doubt about the cost savings that employers can enjoy by including PAs on their staffs. As studies have shown, PAs generate four to five times their salaries in billing. One recent study indicated that physicians who employ PAs are much more productive in the number of patients they see per week and enjoy a much higher average income than those who do not use PAs. But even more important, PAs' training, qualifications, and experience ensure that they will, in the words of the Congressional Office of Technical Assessment, "provide care that is the equivalent in quality to the care provided by physicians."

Taken as a whole, all of these factors suggest a bright future for PAs for years to come.

Appendix A

Community Scholarship Programs

STATES CURRENTLY PARTICIPATING in community scholarship programs include the following:

Alabama
State Health Planning and Development Agency
125 South Ripley Street, Suite 1
Montgomery, AL 36130

Kentucky
Cabinet for Human Resources
275 East Main Street
Frankfort, KY 40065

Nevada
Office of Rural Health
Room 201 (150)
Reno, NV 89557-0046

North Carolina
North Carolina Department of Human Resources
Office of Rural Health and Resource Development
311 Ashe Avenue
Raleigh, NC 27606

South Carolina
Medical University of South Carolina
171 Ashley Avenue
Charleston, SC 29424

West Virginia
Research Corporation for West Virginia University
213 Glennlock Hall
Morgantown, WV 26506

Appendix B

Physician Assistant and Related Organizations

Accreditation Review Committee on Education for Physician
  Assistants
1000 North Oak Street
Marshfield, WI 54449-5788

American Academy of Nurse Practitioners
National Administrative Office
P.O. Box 12846
Austin, TX 78711

American Academy of Physician Assistants
950 North Washington Street
Alexandria, VA 22314-1552

American Association of Nurse Anesthetists
222 South Project Avenue
Park Ridge, IL 60068

American College of Nurse Midwives
818 Connecticut Avenue NW
Washington, D.C. 20006

Association of Physician Assistant Programs
950 North Washington Street
Alexandria, VA 22314-1552

National Commission on Certification of Physician Assistants, Inc.
157 Technology Parkway, Suite 800
Norcross, GA 30092-2913

Society of Dermatology Physician Assistants
7441 South Atlantic Avenue
Tulsa, OK 74136

Society of Emergency Medicine Physician Assistants
950 North Washington Street
Alexandria, VA 22314-1552

Society for Physician Assistants in Pediatrics
950 North Washington Street
Alexandria, VA 22314-1552

APPENDIX C

Physician Assistant Training Programs

THE PROGRAMS LISTED here are accredited by the Accreditation Review Commission on Education for physician assistants. Several new programs are also in the process of being accredited. Contact the college or university of your choice for up-to-date information.

Alabama

University of Alabama at Birmingham
Surgical Physician Assistant Program
School of Health Related Professions
SHR2 Annex 1530, Third Avenue South
Birmingham, AL 35294-1270

University of South Alabama
Department of Physician Assistant Studies
1504 Springhill Avenue, Room 4410
Mobile, AL 36604-3273

Arizona

Arizona School of Health Sciences
Kirksville College of Osteopathic Medicine
Physician Assistant Program
3210 West Camelback Road
Phoenix, AZ 85017

Midwestern University
Physician Assistant Program
19555 North Fifty-ninth Avenue
Glendale, AZ 85308

California

Charles R. Drew University of Medicine
    and Science
Physician Assistant Program
College of Health Sciences
1731 East 120th Street
Los Angeles, CA 90059

Loma Linda University
Physician Assistant Program
School of Allied Health Professions
Nichol Hall, Room 2033
Loma Linda, CA 92350

Riverside County Regional Medical Center/Riverside
    Community College
Primary Care PA Program
16130 Lasselle Street
Moreno Valley, CA 92551-2045

Samuel Merritt College
Physician Assistant Program
370 Hawthorne Avenue
Oakland, CA 94609

Stanford University School of Medicine
Primary Care Associate Program
703 Welch Road, Suite F-1
Palo Alto, CA 94304-1760

University of California-Davis, Medical Center
Physician Assistant Program/Family Nurse Practitioner Program
Department of Family & Community Medicine
2516 Stockton Boulevard, Suite 254
Sacramento, CA 95817

University of Southern California
Keek School of Medicine
Primary Care Physician Assistant Program
1975 Zonal Avenue, KAM B-29
Los Angeles, CA 90089

Western University of Health Sciences
Physician Assistant Program
College Plaza
Pomona, CA 91766-1854

Colorado

Red Rocks Community College
Physician Assistant Program
13300 West Eighth Avenue
Campus Box 38
Lakewood, CO 80228-1255

University of Colorado
Child Health Associate/PA Program
School of Medicine
Box C-219
4200 East Ninth Avenue
Denver, CO 80262

Connecticut

Quinnipiac University
Physician Assistant Program
Office of Graduate Admissions
Hamden, CT 06518-1908

Yale University
Physician Assistant Program
School of Medicine
47 College Street, Suite 220
New Haven, CT 06510

District of Columbia

George Washington University
Physician Assistant Program
2175 K Street NW, Suite 820
Washington, D.C. 20037

Howard University
Department of Physician Assistant
College of Allied Health Sciences
Sixth & Bryant Streets NW,
    Annex 1
Washington, D.C. 20059

Florida

Barry University
Physician Assistant Program
School of Graduate Medical Sciences
11300 Northeast Second Avenue
Miami Shores, FL 33161-6695

Miami-Dade Community College
Physician Assistant Program
Medical Center Campus
950 NW Twentieth Street
Miami, FL 33127-4693

Nova Southeastern University
Physician Assistant Program
3200 South University Drive
Fort Lauderdale, FL 33328

University of Florida
Physician Assistant Program
P.O. Box 100176
Gainesville, FL 32610-0176

Georgia

Emory University School of Medicine
Physician Assistant Program
1462 Clifton Road NE, Suite 280
Atlanta, GA 30322

Medical College of Georgia
Physician Assistant Department
AE 1032
Augusta, GA 30912

South College Physician Assistant Program
9 Mall Court
Savannah, GA 31406

Idaho

Idaho State University
Physician Assistant Program
Campus Box 8253
Pocatello, ID 83208-8253

Illinois

Cook County Hospital/Malcolm X College
Physician Assistant Program
1900 West Van Buren Street
Suite #3241
Chicago, IL 60612

Finch University of Health Sciences
The Chicago Medical School
3333 Green Bay Road, Building #51
North Chicago, IL 60064-3095

Midwestern University
Physician Assistant Program
555 West Thirty-first Street
Downers Grove, IL 60515

Southern Illinois University
Physician Assistant Program
Lindegren Hall, Room 129 MC 6516
Carbondale, IL 62901-6516

Indiana

Butler University/Clarian Health
Physician Assistant Program
College of Pharmacy & Health Sciences
4600 Sunset Avenue
Indianapolis, IN 46208

University of Saint Francis
Physician Assistant Program
2701 Spring Street
Fort Wayne, IN 46808

Iowa

Des Moines University–Osteopathic Medical Center
Physician Assistant Program
3200 Grand Avenue
Des Moines, IA 50912

University of Iowa
Physician Assistant Program
College of Medicine
5167 Westlawn
Iowa City, IA 52242

Kansas

Wichita State University
Physician Assistant Program
College of Health Professions
Campus Box 43
Wichita, KS 67260

Kentucky

University of Kentucky
Physician Assistant Program
121 Washington Avenue, Room 118
Lexington, KY 40536-0003

Louisiana

Louisiana State University Health Science Center
Physician Assistant Program
School of Allied Health Professions
1501 Kings Highway, P.O. Box 33932
Shreveport, LA 71130

Maine

The University of New England
Physician Assistant Program
11 Hills Beach Road
Biddeford, ME 04005

Maryland

Anne Arundel Community College
Physician Assistant Program
School of Health Professions, Wellness and
    Physician Education
101 College Parkway
Arnold, MD 21012

Community College of Baltimore—Essex Campus
Physician Assistant Program
7201 Rossville Boulevard
Baltimore, MD 21237

University of Maryland—Eastern Shore
Physician Assistant Program
Modular 934-5 Backbone Road
Princess Anne, MD 21853

Massachusetts

Massachusetts College of Pharmacy
Physician Assistant Program
179 Longwood Avenue, WB01
Boston, MA 02115

Springfield College/Baystate Health System
Physician Assistant Program
253 Alden Street
Springfield, MA 01109

Michigan

Central Michigan University
Physician Assistant Program
Foust Hall
Mount Pleasant, MI 48859

Grand Valley State University
Physician Assistant Program
Medical Education & Research Center
251 Michigan Street NE
Grand Rapids, MI 59503

University of Detroit-Mercy
Physician Assistant Program
8200 West Outer Drive
P.O. Box 19900
Detroit, MI 48219-0900

Wayne State University
Department of Physician Assistant Studies
College of Pharmacy & Allied Health Professions
Detroit, MI 48202

Western Michigan University
Physician Assistant Program
Kalamazoo, MI 49008-5138

Minnesota

Augsburg College
Physician Assistant Program
2211 Riverside Avenue
Campus Box 149
Minneapolis, MN 55454

Missouri

Saint Louis University
Physician Assistant Program
School of Allied Health Professions
3437 Carolline Street
St. Louis, MO 63104

Southwest Missouri State
Physician Assistant Program
901 South National Avenue
Springfield, MO 65804-0089

Montana

Rocky Mountain College
Physician Assistant Program
1511 Poly Drive
Billings, MT 59102-1796

Nebraska

Union College
Physician Assistant Program
9800 South Forty-eighth Street
Lincoln, NE 68506

University of Nebraska Medical Center
Physician Assistant Program
984300 Nebraska Medical Center
Omaha, NE 68198-4300

New Hampshire

Notre Dame College
Physician Assistant Studies
Office of Graduate Admissions and Continuing
    Education
2521 Elm Street
Manchester, NH 03104-2299

New Jersey

Seton Hall University
Physician Assistant Program
400 South Orange Avenue
South Orange, NJ 07079-2689

The University of Medicine and Dentistry of
    New Jersey
Physician Assistant Program
65 Bergen Street
Newark, NJ 07107-3001

University of Medicine and Dentistry of New Jersey
and Rutgers University
Physician Assistant Program
Robert Wood Johnson Medical School
675 Hoes Lane
Piscataway, NJ 08854-5635

New Mexico

University of New Mexico
School of Medicine
Physician Assistant Program
Department of Family & Community Medicine
2400 Tucker NE
Albuquerque, NM 87131-5241

University of St. Francis
Physician Assistant Program
4401 Silver Avenue SE, Suite B
Albuquerque, NM 87108

New York

Albany-Hudson Valley
Physician Assistant Program
Albany Medical College
47 New Scotland Avenue, MC4
Albany, NY 12208

Bronx Lebanon Hospital Center
Physician Assistant Program
1650 Selwyn Avenue, Suite 11D
Bronx, NY 10457

The Brooklyn Hospital Center
Long Island University
Physician Assistant Program
121 DeKalb Avenue
Brooklyn, NY 11201

Cornell University Medical College
Physician Assistant Program
"A Surgical Focus"
1300 York Avenue, F-1919
New York, NY 10021

CUNY/Harlem Hospital Center
Physician Assistant Program
506 Malcolm X Boulevard (aka Lenox Avenue),
    WP-Room 619
New York, NY 10037

Daeman College
Physician Assistant Program
4380 Main Street
Amherst, NY 14226-3592

D'Youville College
Physician Assistant Program
320 Porter Avenue
Buffalo, NY 14201

LeMoyne College
Physician Assistant Program
Department of Biology
1419 Salt Springs Road
Syracuse, NY 13214-1399

Mercy College
Physician Assistant Studies
Graduate Program
555 Broadway
Dobbs Ferry, NY 10522

New York Institute of Technology
Physician Assistant Program
P.O. Box 8000
Old Westbury
New York, NY 11568-8000

Pace University
Lenox Hill Hospital
Physician Assistant Program
1 Pace Plaza
New York, NY 10098

Rochester Institute of Technology
Physician Assistant Program
85 Lomb Memorial Drive
Rochester, NY 14523-5603

St. Vincent Catholic Medical Centers of
    Brooklyn and Queens
Physician Assistant Program
175-05 Horace Harding Expressway
Fresh Meadows, NY 11365

St. Vincent Catholic Medical Centers
    of New York
Physician Assistant Program
75 Vanderbilt Avenue
Staten Island, NY 10304

State University of New York at Stony Brook
Physician Assistant Program
School of Health Technology & Management
HSC L2-052
Stony Brook, NY 11794-8202

Tonro College
Physician Assistant Program
School of Health Sciences
1700 Union Boulevard
Bay Shore, NY 11706

Tonro College
Physician Assistant Program
Manhattan Campus
27-33 West Twenty-third Street
New York, NY 10010

Wagner College/Staten Island University Hospital
Physician Assistant Program
74 Melville Street
Staten Island, NY 10309-4035

North Carolina

Duke University Medical Center
Physician Assistant Program
DUMC 3848
Durham, NC 27710

East Carolina University
Physician Assistant Program
School of Allied Health Sciences
Carol Belk Building, Annex 6
Greenville, NC 27858-4363

Methodist College
Physician Assistant Program
5400 Ramsey Street
Fayetteville, NC 28311

Wake Forest University Baptist Medical Center
Physician Assistant Program
School of Medicine
1990 Beach Street
Winston-Salem, NC 27103

North Dakota

University of North Dakota School of Medicine &
    Health Sciences
Physician Assistant Program
Department of Community Medicine and Rural
    Health
P.O. Box 9037
Grand Forks, ND 58202-9037

Ohio

Cuyahoga Community College
Physician Assistant Program
11000 Pleasant Valley Road
Parma, OH 44130

Kettering College of Medical Arts
Physician Assistant Program
3737 Southern Boulevard
Kettering, OH 46429

Medical College of Ohio
Physician Assistant Program
School of Allied Health
3015 Arlington Avenue
Toledo, OH 43614-5803

University of Findlay
Physician Assistant Program
1000 North Main Street
Findlay, OH 45840

Oklahoma

University of Oklahoma
Physician Assistant Program
Health Sciences Center
P.O. Box 26901
Oklahoma City, OK 73190

Oregon

Oregon Health Sciences University
Physician Assistant Program
3181 SW Sam Jackson Park Road
GH219
Portland, OR 97201-3098

Pacific University
School of Physician Assistant Studies
2043 College Way
Forest Grove, OR 97116

Pennsylvania

Beaver College
Physician Assistant Program
Brubaker Hall, Health Science Center
450 South Easton Road
Glenside, PA 19038-3295

Chatham College
Physician Assistant Program
Woodland Road
Pittsburgh, PA 16232

DeSales University
Physician Assistant Program
2755 Station Avenue
Center Valley, PA 18034-9568

Duquesne University
Department of Physician Assistant
John G. Rangos, Sr., School of Health Sciences
323 Health Sciences Building
Pittsburgh, PA 15282

Gannon University
Physician Assistant Program
109 University Square
Erie, PA 16541

King's College
Physician Assistant Program
133 North River Street
Wilkes-Barre, PA 18711

Lock Haven University of Pennsylvania
Physician Assistant in Rural Primary Care Program
Lock Haven, PA 17745

Marywood University
Physician Assistant Program
2300 Adams Avenue
Scranton, PA 18509

MCP Hahnemann University
Physician Assistant Program
College of Nursing & Health Professions
Mail Stop 504
245 North Sixteenth Street
Philadelphia, PA 19102-1192

Pennsylvania College of Technology
Physician Assistant Program
One College Avenue, DIF #123
Williamsport, PA 17701-5799

Philadelphia College of Osteopathic Medicine
Department of Physician Assistant Studies
4170 City Avenue, Suite 005
Evans Hall
Philadelphia, PA 19131

Philadelphia University
Physician Assistant Program
School House Lane & Henry Avenue
Philadelphia, PA 19144

Saint Francis University
Physician Assistant Program
P.O. Box 600
Loretto, PA 15940-0600

Seton Hill College
Physician Assistant Program
College Avenue
Greensburg, PA 15601

South Carolina

Medical University of South Carolina
Physician Assistant Program
College of Health Professions
P.O. Box 250856
Charleston, SC 29425-2703

South Dakota

University of South Dakota
Physician Assistant Studies
School of Medicine
414 East Clark Street
Vermillion, SD 57069-2390

Tennessee

Bethel College
Physician Assistant Program
325 Cherry Avenue
McKenzie, TN 38201

Treveoca Nazarene University
Physician Assistant Program
333 Murfreesboro Road
Nashville, TN 37210-2877

Texas

Baylor College of Medicine
Physician Assistant Program
One Baylor Plaza, Room 633E
Houston, TX 77030

Texas Tech University Health Sciences Center
Physician Assistant Program
School of Allied Health
Department of Diagnostic & Primary Care
3600 North Garfield
Midland, TX 79706

Uniformed Services
Interservice Physician Assistant Program
Academy of Health Sciences
Attn: MCCS-HMP (PA Branch)
3151 Scott Road, Suite 1202
Fort Sam Houston, TX 78234-6138

University of North Texas Health Science Center at
    Fort Worth
Physician Assistant Program
3600 Camp Bowie Boulevard
Fort Worth, TX 76107

The University of Texas Health Science Center
  at San Antonio
Physician Assistant Studies
7703 Floyd Curl Drive, MC 6249
San Antonio, TX 78229

The University of Texas Medical Branch
Physician Assistant Program
School of Allied Health Services
301 University Boulevard
Galveston, TX 77555-1028

The University of Texas-Pan American
Physician Assistant Program
1201 West University Drive
Edinburg, TX 78539-2999

University of Texas Southwestern Medical
  Center at Dallas
Physician Assistant Program
6011 Harry Hines Boulevard
Dallas, TX 75390-9090

Utah

University of Utah
Physician Assistant Program
School of Medicine
50 North Medical Drive, Building 528
Salt Lake City, UT 84132

Virginia

College of Health Sciences
Physician Assistant Program
920 South Jefferson Street
Roanoke, VA 24016

Eastern Virginia Medical School
Physician Assistant Program
700 West Olney Road, P.O. Box 1980
Norfolk, VA 23501-1980

James Madison University
Physician Assistant Program
Department of Health Science
MSC 4301
Harrisonburg, VA 23807

Washington

University of Washington
MEDEX/Northwest
Physician Assistant Program
4245 Roosevelt Way NE
Seattle, WA 98105-6920

West Virginia

Alderson Broaddus College
Physician Assistant Program
Box 2036
Philippi, WV 26416

The College of West Virginia
Physician Assistant Program
P.O. Box AG
Beckley, WV 25802

Wisconsin

Marquette University
Physician Assistant Program
College of Health Sciences
1700 Building
P.O. Box 1881
Milwaukee, WI 53201-1881

University of Wisconsin
LaCrosse-Gunderson Lutheran Medical
    Foundation
Physician Assistant Program
Mayo School of Health Related Sciences
4031 Health Science Center
1725 State Street
LaCrosse, WI 54601-3767

University of Wisconsin—Madison
Physician Assistant Program
Room 1050 Medical Sciences Center
1300 University Avenue
Madison, WI 53706

Appendix D

AAPA Constituent Societies

Society of Air Force PAs
950 North Washington Street
Alexandria, VA 22314-1552

Alabama Society of PAs
P.O. Box 550274
Birmingham, AL 35255-0274

Alaska Academy of PAs
P.O. Box 74187
Fairbanks, AK 99707-4187
E-mail: akapa@mosquitonet.com

Arizona State Association of PAs
P.O. Box 12307
Glendale, AZ 85318

Arkansas Academy of PAs
950 North Washington Street
Alexandria, VA 22314-1552

Society of Army PAs
6762 Candlewood Drive
Ft. Myers, FL 33919-6402

California Academy of PAs
3100 West Warner Avenue, Suite 3
Santa Ana, CA 92704-5331
E-mail: capa@capanet.org

Colorado Academy of PAs
P.O. Box 4834
Englewood, CO 80155-4834

Connecticut Academy of PAs
P.O. Box 81362
Wellesley, MA 02481-0004

Delaware Academy of PAs
704 Dorcaster Drive
Wilmington, DE 19808-2214

District of Colombia Academy of PAs
Techworld Station
P.O. Box 50147
800 K Street NW
Washington, D.C. 20091-9998
E-mail: neurosurgpa@msn.com

Downeast Association of PAs
P.O. Box 2027
Augusta, ME 04338-2027

Florida Academy of PAs
222 South Westmonte Drive, Suite 101
Altamonte Springs, FL 32714

Georgia Association of PAs
980 Canton Street, Building 1,
  Suite B
Roswell, GA 30075
E-mail: gapa@gapaonline.org

Guahan Association of PAS
P.O. Box 6578
Tamuning, GU 96911

Hawaii Academy of PAs
P.O. Box 30355
Honolulu, HI 96820-0355
E-mail: hapa@aapa.org

Idaho Academy of PAs
P.O. Box 2668
305 West Jefferson
Boise, ID 83701

Illinois Academy of PAs
625 South Second Street
Springfield, IL 62704
E-mail: iapa@ampka.com

Indiana Academy of PAs
950 North Washington Street
Alexandria, VA 22314-1552
E-mail: iapa@aapa.org

Iowa PA Society
200 Tenth Street, 5th Floor
Des Moines, IA 50309
E-mail: ipas@metins.net

Kansas Academy of PAs
P.O. Box 597
Topeka, KS 66601

Kentucky Academy of PAs
P.O. Box 23251
Lexington, KY 40523-3251

Louisiana Academy of PAs
8550 United Plaza Boulevard, Suite 1001
Baton Rouge, LA 70809
E-mail: lapa@pncpa.com

Maryland Academy of PAs
P.O. Box 20277
Baltimore, MD 21284
E-mail: info@mdapa.org

Massachusetts Association of PAs
950 North Washington Street
Alexandria, VA 22314-1552
E-mail: mass-pas@aapa.org

Michigan Academy of PAs
120 West Saginaw Street
P.O. Box 950
East Lansing, MI 48823
E-mail: mapa@msms.org

Minnesota Academy of PAs
3433 Broadway Street NE, Suite 300
Minneapolis, MN 55413-1761
E-mail: mapa@mnmed.org

Mississippi Academy of PAs
P.O. Box 5128
Biloxi, MS 39534-0128
E-mail: missipas@aapa.org

Missouri Academy of PAs
950 North Washington Street
Alexandria, VA 22314-1552
E-mail: mapa@aapa.org

Montana Academy of PAs
1720 Ninth Avenue
Helena, MT 59601
E-mail: mapa@mtha.org

Naval Association
950 North Washington Street
Alexandria, VA 22314-1552
E-mail: napa@aapa.org

Nebraska Academy of PAs
7906 Davenport
Omaha, NE 68114

Nevada Academy of PAs
P.O. Box 28877
Las Vegas, NV 89126-2877

New Hampshire Society of PAs
P.O. Box 325
Manchester, NH 00310

New Jersey State Society of PAs
P.O. Box 1282
Piscataway, NJ 08855-1282
E-mail: njsspa@njsspa.org

New Mexico Academy of PAs
160 Washington Street SE, Box 1
Albuquerque, NM 87108
E-mail: nmpa@nmapa.com

New York State Society of PAs
322 Eighth Avenue, Suite 1400
New York, NY 10001-8001

North Carolina Academy of PAs
3209 Guess Road, Suite 105
Durham, NC 27705
E-mail: ncapa@mindspring.com

North Dakota Academy of PAs
MSU Campus
Box 91
Minot, ND 58707

Ohio Association of PAs
4683 Winterset Drive
Columbus, OH 43220
E-mail: oapa@infinet.com

Oklahoma Academy of PAs
P.O. Box 53164
Oklahoma City, OK 73152

Oregon Society of PAs
P.O. Box 514
Oregon City, OR 97045-0029
E-mail: ospas@aol.com

Pennsylvania Society of PAs
P.O. Box 128
Greensburg, PA 15601-0128
E-mail: pspa@usaor.net

Public Health Service APA
950 North Washington Street
Alexandria, VA 22314-1552
E-mail: phs@aapa.org

Rhode Island Academy of PAs
106 Francis Street
Providence, RI 02908
E-mail: riapa@aol.com

South Carolina Academy of PAs
P.O. Box 1452
Columbia, SC 29202
E-mail: association@sc.rr.com

South Dakota Academy of PAs
3708 Brooks Place, Suite 1
Sioux Falls, SD 57106-4211

Tennessee Academy of PAs
1483 North Mt. Juliet Road, PMB #203
Mt. Juliet, TN 37122
E-mail: tapadirector@msn.com

Texas Academy of PAs
401 West Fifteenth Street
Austin, TX 78701-1680

Utah Academy of PAs
50 North Medical Drive, Building 528
Salt Lake City, UT 84132

PAs Academy of Vermont
68 Overlook Drive
South Burlington, VT 05403
E-mail: paav@cyberportal.net

Veterans Affairs PA Association
950 North Washington Street
Alexandria, VA 22314-1552
E-mail: vapaa@aapa.org

Virginia Academy of PAs
10301 Democracy Lane, Suite 203
Fairfax, VA 22030
E-mail: vapa@vapa.org

Washington State APA
620B Industry Drive, Building 8
Tukwila, WA 98188-3406
E-mail: wapa123@aol.com

West Virginia Assn. of PAs
P.O. Box 3625
Charleston, WV 25336-3625
E-mail: wvapa@aapa.org

Wisconsin Academy of PAs
P.O. Box 1109
Madison, WI 53701-1109
E-mail: wapa@smswi.org

Wyoming Association of PAs
1260-62 West Fifth Street
Sheridan, WY 82801

Specialty Organizations

AAPAs in Allergy, Asthma, and Immunology
10470 Vista Del Sol, #100
El Paso, TX 79925
E-mail: aapaai99@netscape.net

American Academy of Nephrology PAs
245 Sugar Pine Drive
Pinehurst, NC 28374

American Academy of PAs in Occupational Medicine
9712 Old Kay Road, Suite 102
Houston, TX 77055
E-mail: aapa-om@texres.com

American Association for Plastic and Reconstructive Surgery PAs
252-24 Eighty-second Drive
Bellerose, NY 11426-2509

American Association of Surgical PAs
P.O. Box 867
Bernardsville, NJ 07924
E-mail: theaaspa@aol.com

American Society of Endocrine PAs
950 North Washington Street
Alexandria, VA 22314-1552
E-mail: asepa@mailcity.com

Association of Family Practice PAs
7443 Legend Point Drive
San Antonio, TX 78244-2412
E-mail: afppa@aol.com

Association of Neurological PAs
P.O. Box 559
Bernardsville, NJ 07924
E-mail: neuropac@aol.com

Association of PAs in Cardiovascular
    Surgery
P.O. Box 4834
Englewood, CO 80111

Association of PAs in Obstetrics &
    Gynecology
P.O. Box 1109
Madison, WI 53701-1109

Association of PAs in Oncology
3408 Reynoldswood Drive
Tampa, FL 33618-2114

Association of Psychiatric PAs
P.O. Box 1041
Rusk, TX 75785
E-mail: whkh@tyler.net

PAs in Orthopedic Surgery
P.O. Box 10781
Glendale, AZ 85318-0781

Society of Dermatology PAs
6218 East Seventy-eighth Street
Tulsa, OK 74136

Society of Emergency Medicine PAs
950 North Washington Street
Alexandria, VA 22314-1552
E-mail: info@sempa.org

Society of PAs in Addiction Medicine
1157 Union Lake Road
White Lake, MI 48386-4348

Society of PAs Caring for the Elderly
P.O. Box 639
Lizella, GA 31052

Society of PAs in Otolaryngology/Head & Neck Surgery
950 North Washington
Alexandria, VA 22314-1552

Society for PAs in Pediatrics
950 North Washington Street
Alexandria, VA 22314-1552

Urological Association of PAs
University of South Alabama
Department of PA Studies
1504 Springhill Avenue, Suite 4410
Mobile, AL 36604

Caucuses

African Heritage Caucus
9334 Scenic Mountain Lane
Las Vegas, NV 89117

Caduceus Caucus
2215 Vintage Drive W
Colorado Springs, CO 80920-3809

Correctional Medicine Caucus
4102 Seventieth Street
Lubbock, TX 79413-5920

Fellowship of Christian PAs
950 North Washington Street
Alexandria, VA 22314-1552

First Nations Caucus of PAs
14014 NW Passage, No. 342
Marina Del Rey, CA 90292-7427

Lesbian, Bisexual, and Gay PA Caucus
1803 North Warren Avenue
Milwaukee, WI 53202

PA AIDS Network
1717 Burnell Drive
Los Angeles, CA 90065

PAs of Asians and Pacific Islanders
1102 Bates, Suite 1150 MC3-2371
Houston, TX 77030

PAs for Cross-Cultural Involvement
P.O. Box 1252
Huntington Beach, CA 92647

PAs of Latino Heritage
950 North Washington Street
Alexandria, VA 22314-1552

PAs Pilots Caucus
4916 East Wagner Road
Scottsdale, AZ 85254

Rural Health Caucus of the AAPA
1013 First Street, Box C
Redfield, IA 50233-0903

Veterans Caucus of the AAPA
100 North Academy Avenue
Danville, PA 17822-1350

Bibliography

Books

Annotated Bibliography of the Physician Assistant Program. Alexandria, VA: American Academy of Physician Assistants, 2001.

Birchenall, Joan A. and Mary Eileen Straight. *Health Occupations: Exploration and Career Planning.* St. Louis: C. V. Mosby Co., 1992.

Health Care in Rural America. Washington, D.C.: Superintendent of Documents, U.S. Government Printing Office, 1990.

Kacen, A. *Opportunities in Paramedical Careers.* Chicago: VGM Career Books, 1999.

Physician Assistant Legal Handbook. Alexandria, VA: American Academy of Physician Assistants, 2001.

Physician Assistant Programs Directory, 19th Ed. Alexandria, VA: Association of Physician Assistant Programs, 2000.

Physician Assistant Student Financial Aid Booklet. Alexandria,
VA: American Academy of Physician Assistants, 2001.

Physician Assistants: Statistics and Trends, 1991–1998.
Alexandria, VA: American Academy of Physician
Assistants, 1999.

Sacks, Terence J. *Careers in Medicine.* Chicago: VGM Career
Books, 1997.

———. *Careers in Nursing.* Chicago: VGM Career Books,
1998.

———. *Opportunities in Osteopathic Medicine Careers.* Chicago:
VGM Career Books, 2001.

Snook, Jr., I. Donald, and Leo D'Orazio. *Opportunities in
Health and Medical Careers.* Chicago: VGM Career Books,
1991.

Swanson, Barbara. *Careers in Healthcare* (Physician Assistant,
Chapter 5). Chicago: VGM Career Books, 1989.

Articles

Appleby, Chuck. "Boxed in." *Hospitals and Health Networks.*
Vol. 69, (September 20, 1995).

"Docs vs. Mini-Docs." *Wall Street Journal.* (September 1992).

Estes, MD, E. Harvey. "The PA Experiment After 25 Years:
What Have We Learned?" *Journal of the American Academy
of Physician Assistants* (October 1992).

"Filling the Gap: Mid-Level Practitioners Provide Healthcare in
Areas Shunned by Physicians." *Modern Health Care.* (May
13, 1991).

"Home Care and Physician Assistants." *Journal of the American
Medical Association.* 264 (August 8, 1990).

Khanna, Perna Mona. "While Physician Extenders Proliferate, Doctors Worry About Competition." *Wall Street Journal.* (August 9, 1992).

Larkin, Howard. "Physician Assistant: Rx for Stress." *American Medical News.* (March 25, 1991).

"Nurses Chart a New Course." Med-Life Section. *Chicago Sun-Times.* (May 3, 1993).

"Nurses to Recommend Provider Mix in Shortage Areas." *Public Health Reports.* (January-February 1998).

"Physician Assistants Lend a Thrifty Hand." *Wall Street Journal.* (July 18, 1990).

"Physician Assistants and Nurse Practitioners in Hospital Outpatient Departments." *Public Health Reports.* (January-February 1998).

Safriet, B. "Health Care Dollars and Regulatory Sense: The Role of Advanced Practice Nursing." *Yale Journal on Regulation.* (Summer 1992).

"Satisfaction of Physician Assistants and Other Non-Physician Providers in a Managed Care Setting." *Public Health Reports.* (November-December 1998).

Stanhope, William D. PA-C. "The Role of the American Academy of Physician Assistants. *Journal of the American Academy of Physician Assistants.* 5 (October 1992).

Ventura, Marissa and Deborah Grandinetti. "Nurse Physician Report: A Survey," *RN.* Vol. 62 (July 1999).

Pamphlets and Information

Basic Facts About Certified Nurse-Midwives. Washington, D.C.: American College of Nurse Midwives, 1992.

Certified Nurse-Midwives: Careers and Background Rich in Diversity. Washington, D.C.: American College of Nurse Midwives, 1993.

Lauffer MS, PA-Cl., Daniel. "Physician Assistant: An Overview." *The Continental RX.* Vol. 13, No. 2, Winter 1991.

Medex Northwest—Physician Assistant Training Program. Seattle: School of Public Health, University of Washington, 1993.

Nurse Midwives Historically Key to Maternal Healthcare Problems. Washington, D.C.: American College of Nurse-Midwives, 1993.

Nurse Practitioners, Physician Assistants and Certified Nurse Midwives: A Policy Analysis. HCS 37, Congress of the United States Office of Technology Assessment, December 1986.

Nursing Facts. Washington, D.C.: American Nurses Association, 1999.

Physician Assistant. Minneapolis: The Finney Co., Vol. VI, November 8, 1991.

Physician Assistant. *Occupational Outlook Handbook.* Washington, D.C.: Bureau of Labor Statistics, 2000.

Physician Assistant Student Financial Aid Booklet. Alexandria, VA: American Academy of Physician Assistants, 2000.

Physician Assistant and Surgeon Assistant Directory of Medical Education Programs. Chicago: Division of Allied Health Education and Accreditation, American Medical Association, 1992.

Physician Assistants: Partners in Medicine. Alexandria, VA: American Academy of Physician Assistants, 2000.

"Report of the National Survey of the American Academy of Nurse Practitioners." Austin, TX: *Journal of the American Academy of Nurse Practitioners*, January-March 1991.

Scope of Practice for Nurse Practitioners. Austin, TX: American Academy of Nurse Practitioners, 1992.

2000 AAPA Physician Assistants Census Report. Alexandria, VA: American Academy of Physician Assistants, 2000.

ABOUT THE AUTHOR

TERENCE J. SACKS IS an independent writer-editor with more than twenty-five years' experience in communications. During that period he has written dozens of news stories, magazine articles, and speeches. Sacks's articles have appeared in such publications as *Hospitals* and *Chicago Medicine*.

Sacks, a graduate of Northwestern University's Medill School of Journalism, has strong credentials in the field of health care. From 1970 to 1973 he was director of communications for the Chicago Medical Society, the local professional group for physicians in Chicago and Cook County. He has also held positions in communications for the American Osteopathic Association, the American Association of Dental Schools, and for several hospitals in Chicago.

Sacks is currently on the journalism faculty of Columbia College in Chicago, where he teaches "Introduction to the Mass Media." At Columbia he also has taught courses in news reporting, feature writing, editing company publications, and the history of journalism.

For the past fifteen years, Sacks has headed his own writing and communications firm, Terence J. Sacks Associates. He is active in the Independent Writers of Chicago (where he is also on the board), the American Medical Writers Association, and the Publicity Club of Chicago.

His daughter, Lili, is a physician specializing in internal medicine in Seattle and has been most helpful in the completion of this manuscript.